Star Status Publishing

Presents

I0201023

TALES OF AN ORIGINAL BAD GIRL
AN AUTOBIOGRAPHY

(*An* Autobiography of an O.B.G)

BY:

Mack Mama

Star Status Publishing
P.O Box 237
Derby CT 06418
www.mackmamamentor.com

= =

Tales of an Original Bad Girl
Copyright © 2011 by Mack Mama

ISBN-10: 0-9831178-4-5

ISBN-13: 978-0-9831178-4-1

Paperback Edition, 2012

Manufactured in the United States of America

REVISED PRINT, Second Edition 2012

Designed by Dashawn Taylor

Typesetting: HotBookCovers.com

Editor: James "Shaquell" Forbes

What other Authors are saying about

"TALES OF AN ORIGINAL BAD GIRL"

BY:

Mack Mama

"I finished reading this memoir feeling like I know Mack Mama she bared her soul it was refreshing and very raw"....Dashawn Taylor author of From Poverty to Power Moves and The Kissed by the Devil – Book Series

"Tales of an Original Bad Girl is one of the best books I've read this year. It's inspirational, entertaining, controversial and definitely a page turner. You won't be able to put this one down" . Miz author of Bishop, Bulldog Crew, and Haters Animosity.

"It's amazing to me how I was able to use two voices in this memoir. The voice of reason and the voice of insanity"......Mack Mama author of Daisy Jones.

"Mack Mama is the real McCoy, a genuine lady 'G' who tells a tumultuous tale that will have readers ripping through pages and shaking their heads in disbelief. Brooklyn born, Natoka "Mack Mama" Williams was reared in an urban hell where narcotics, betrayals, abandonment and violence were the norm. Little Natoka's parents were both heroin addicts but conditions quickly deteriorated after her mother contracted AIDS. Natoka went from an A student in a school for the gifted to one of New York's most notorious female desperados. Mack Mama slipped seamlessly from selling crack for the bloody Brooklyn gunslinger Fifty Cent, to the theft of high-end merchandise, to pimping, to organizing a credit card fraud ring, and shooting anyone who got in her way. Even prison couldn't quell the Mack's lust for a lavish lifestyle, she was all or nothing and she feared no wrath. She truly is an original bad girl." Cavario H editor of Hip Hop Weekly and author of "Raised by Wolves".

DEDICATION

I dedicate this Memoir to the memory of both my beloved mother **Gaynelle Williams,** and my godmother **Louise A. Robinson**. Without these two women I would not have been able to write my story.

My mother gave me life and my godmother nourished that life. I also dedicate this book to my Grandmother **Janie "Nana" Williams** for constantly being there for me in my time of need. It's comforting to know that I can always call your house my home.

Last but not least to my darling daughter **Velvet G. Washington** so you can use it as a reminder to make the right choices in your life.

I love you all with every beat of my heart!

ACKNOWLEDEMENTS

First and foremost, I have to give praises to my lord and savior Jesus Christ I want you to know that your prodigal daughter will be home soon.

I want to thank my big sister Queenie for always being my rock, and being the greatest godmother on earth. You get the Louise A. Robinson award, and you know that is an honor. I love you and would gladly give you any one of my organs, if you ever needed it. You already have my heart. Eternal!

I love you Nana and I thank you for being there for me whenever I went to jail. You always took my calls and held on to my worldly possessions. You are so important to my life and you're the only mom I have left. I pray all the time that you live to be 104, like your mom did, because Raquele, Velvet and I need you. You're all we have left. p.s. you're a foxy 87 year old lady (smile)

To my lil' sister Raquele, you will always be my baby, and I will always take care of you, like I promised mommy. I love you and am so proud of your accomplishments. I always say "that should have been me". You did it kid! You defied the odds and made a choice to be successful. You are my star. If Queenie and I had big sisters like "us" we would have achieved the academic accomplishments. Like having a Master's Degree and a PHD in Pharmacy like our other little sis Tammy, so that means you two ladies are lucky to have had us, to keep you girls focused (I stole some of the shine back)..lol

To my father Coydine Mackie, I want to say thank you for being a man and taking care of your responsibility when you were able to. I am happy you are in my life and it's never too late to bond. You may not realize how much I love you, but you mean the world to me, and Velvet. You've made up for all the lost time. I couldn't ask for a better dad or friend, for that matter.

I want to thank my partner Kenya "Sparkles" Williams, for restoring my faith in humanity. You were there for me without even knowing me. You are amazing, and I will never let you down, like others have. You went through all the fakers so you could appreciate the real deal baby! I love you till the death...

Velma Williams I love you, thanks for all the times you covered me on the Su-Su. You have embraced me, and my daughter into your family with open arms, and a loving heart. I don't know what I would have done without my Connecticut family. Thank you!

Cheryl "Goldie" Samuels I have to give you a standing ovation for your constant loyalty, and love for me. You were there when I was in the midst of my grind and contributed with blind faith, and will be there at the end of the rainbow when I reach my pot of gold. Thank you for loving me so much that you never retaliated, and understanding the actions of a victim of abuse. You will always be my family I love you Turtle.

That brings me to my dear friend, Margaret "Poochie" Monroe. May God's strength bring you out of the fire. I love you and I will always be there for you, as you have been for me. You were there from the start of Mack Mama, I used to wake you up, to come in the bathroom late at night, when we were in Albion, so you could listen to my new songs. I used to be so excited. Remember, you always encouraged me. Thank you, "Poochie", "Diane" and "Margaret". (Smile)

My Paul, I love you and will never forget all of our days on the grind chasing that paper. I didn't tell half of the stories about our escapades on the road, because I didn't want to glorify or teach the kids how to be better criminal. You are way more than my partner in crime you're one of my dearest friends. I will always cherish our memories together. I am so glad you were able to read my book before you passed away. November 13, 2011 a great man and my dearest friend left this earth. Rest in peace! Paul Harnik.

To my brother from another mother Sherm "The Worm" Adams you are a perfect example of change. I love you bro, you inspire me to keep my head up. If you can smile with your situation and, all you have been through than I better laugh like a hyena. Lol

Special Thank you to my fellow authors Miz, and Dashawn Taylor

Miz you are the best and I am blessed to have met you. You are a real dude thanks for always dropping jewels on me about this book game. If you didn't hook me up with Dashawn, I wouldn't be this happy about the outcome of my product. Quality work hands down! You always look out for me, and I consider you my mentor in this biz. I rep you as much as you rep me, believe that!

Thank you Dashawn Taylor for doing such an awesome job designing my book covers. You had so much patience with me, and took your time with my photo gallery, which made it so HOT!! You saw my vision and made it happen. For that I will be forever grateful.

Thank you Gordon O'neil @Metropolust Photography my favorite photographer and friend,

Thank you Super Dave for the great footage all these years ....you guys are the best!

I love all my facebook friends. Thanks for all the positive comments and the love, I have the best fans in the world, and I'm getting more every day. muah! I love you Darlins.

The same love goes out to my Twitter followers. Keep re-tweeting ! Love y'all.

To every underground Artist that is striving for that big break, keep on grinding and paying your dues, regardless how long it takes. Time, nor any obstacles can stop what God has planned for you. I am living proof of that! I'm one of you and I made it!

Free Joseph "Mighty" Jackson! Keep your head up King, thanks for always being there for me. I will never forget our "Sundays"

James "Shaquell" Forbes my comrade, thank you for always trying to find a solution for me to get this book done. I hope it's everything you thought it would be, it's the truth and I stick by it! Thank you very much for taking the time to re-edit this revised version of Tales of an OBG. You are a superb writer and I can't wait to publish our anthology. It's going to be a sizzler!

To Stacy "B.O" Knight congrats on your release, it was long awaited. Love you bro.

Thanks to my newest mentor, Alfred Adams Jr. a.k.a. Shaborn. I am so happy you came into my life. You are so talented and shared so much of your knowledge with me. Love you. Let's get it!

To Walter "TuT" Johnson, you know how I feel about you. I will never be too far away. Loyalty and love!

To all my people on lock down that support me and purchase my (Music, Calendars, Books). I LOVE YOU, work out your body, and your mind. Keep reppin' your girl Mack Mama..cheah!

Thanks to Street Connfinement Magazine, and Buddy for being the first publication to give me some shine when I came home. Shout out to Buddah, you are the best engineer in CT, thanks for all the love y'all show Mack Mama.

Thanks to Cavario H. for being a real dude the most intelligent cat I know. Your words of wisdom are appreciated, and your well wishes for my success.

Shout out to all my girls behind bars, Rikers Island, Bedford Hills, Albion, Taconic, Bayview, York C.I, Danbury Federal and around the world. Use the time to enhance your mind. This incarceration may be a blessing in disguise. I found my talent sitting in a cell. I pray you can too. God Bless!

Special thanks to all the ladies and gents in book clubs across the country, special thanks to: Diamond Eyes Book Club, and Dj Gatsby's book club. You all have supported me and are simply the best! All4One (authors supporting authors) is also a dynamic group on facebook. Founded by Treasure E. Blue (thanks so much Treasure for being such a giving spirit, you really want to see us newbies blow) last but not least my favorite new author Fabiola Joseph creator of Art of Deceit you are a gifted writer, I can't wait to read Porn Stars. Tangie and Daisy must meet soon.

A special acknowledgment to all the fallen Soldiers from Brooklyn New York, rest in peace gone too soon but never forgotten! I miss you Tracy Washington, Velvet would have loved to meet her Uncle. I salute Ja, Bar, Baby Rock, Nubbs from East NY, Fly Ty, ShaSha, Killer Ben, Shuka (killer Ben's lil brother), Juice, JuJu, Fly Ty, Larry "Low Top", Saquon from Crown Heights, Wise from L.G, Pig from Pinkhouses, J.R from L.G, Nut from L.G, Dwayne from L.G ..It's too many to name them all but each and every one of my friends are missed.

To all my homegirls that died from senseless violence or illnesses Rest in peace! Tracy and Baby

Rudy who were brutally stabbed and burned to death, Lil Kisha who was brutally murdered by her boyfriend, Shawn from Lafayette Gardens who was shot and killed, her sister Red who died from an illness at 38, Cruisin who died from a violent fall from a window, Shauna from Fort Greene who was killed by a stray bullet, and all the females worldwide who have died far too young from murder or suicide. I will never forget your lives but for the grace of God it could have been me.

Also make sure you purchase my novel "*DAISY JONES*" and the sequel "*MISTRESS*" also the baby sister to this book "*LESSONS OF AN ORIGINAL BAD GIRL*"

For booking info email: mackmama1@gmail.com

www.mackmamamentor.com

Follow me on www.twitter.com/mackmama

Tune in to my online radio show "Mack Mama's World Radio" on Sundays @ 11:00pm eastern. Call in 424 243-9516 to hear it live on your phone or join the chat room www.blogtalkradio.com/mackmama check out the awesome topics in the archives that you missed and enjoy!

Support my self -titled sound track for this memoir "MACKMAMA" it can be purchased on all the online retailers including www.iTunes.com or www.starstatuspublishing.com all things Mack Mama can be purchased on my company site.

If you received this book without the soundtrack, make sure you purchase the music it will give you the full experience of Tales of an O.B.G

Thanks for supporting Star Status Publishing! It's so hard to keep paper backs alive. Also, please leave a review for all of my books that you have read. If my story inspires you, leave me a testimonial on www.mackmamamentor.com !

Happy Reading People!

TALES OF AN
ORIGINAL
BAD GIRL
AN AUTOBIOGRAPHY

Chapter One

BLOW

This is the story of my life. I was born Natoka Dora Williams to a heroin addicted mother named Gaynelle Williams and a heroin addicted father named Coydine Mackie. I was conceived by two addicts and born into the world addicted to heroin. In the seventies, Children's Services didn't take babies from their parents if they were born with drugs in their system. I wonder if I would have been better off if they had such a policy. Or, maybe, I was dealt the hand that God wanted me to have, because it made me the woman I am today. I made each chapter the title of a song from my soundtrack. My music reflects the life I underwent through the hustle, struggle, pain, fury and triumph. These tales are the truth as I remember them, and I want my readers to judge me not for I have sinned, but love me and pray that I win.

The definition of the word "tales" in the Merriam-Webster Dictionary is as follows: a story for children that involves, but is not limited to, fantastic forces and beings, e.g., fairies, wizards, and goblins.

I used the word "tales" in my title because I wrote my autobiography for the children that are from the ghettos around the world. Some of these children are faced with forces of evil by the allure of street life, and deal with goblins on a daily basis. I grew up dealing with hard-core circumstances that make the belief in fairies and fantasies almost impossible. These are my "Tales of an O.B.G."

As long as I can remember, I had always wanted to blow-up and become rich and famous. I just knew in my heart that rich people didn't have problems, because they seemed happy all of the time. I was a miserable child, but it wasn't due to being mistreated or abused (like most cases). I simply, longed to be with my mother. She raised me, until I was five years old, and then she went to jail. At that point, my godmother, Louise A. Robinson (God rest her sweet soul), took me and my little sister in. That was the last time I lived with my mother until I turned fourteen. I loved my mother fiercely, but I could remember how disappointed and sad I was at times. For example, she would take me into the store while she stole merchandise to support her heroin addiction. Back then, I didn't know she was high off of Heroin when she would take me to the shooting galleries in Harlem with her. My four year old mind would wonder why she and all her friends were always tired and fell asleep while they were standing up. I knew something was fishy, but I couldn't figure it out. I just knew I wanted out of the dirty, smelly apartment, and I was hungry. Although my mother was a drug addict , she was the most loving and fun mother a kid could ever have. She obviously didn't use the best judgment, and was a terrible role model, but that lady loved me, and I felt her love in a tremendous way.

I never forgot the time she took me boosting, and instructed me to block her while she stuffed her bags with clothes. I had to be no more than three years old, but I knew very well that she was doing something wrong, so I told her exactly how I felt. "Mommy, I don't like when you take stuff from the store." I whined.

"Baby, Mommy won't do it again. I just didn't have the money" she would rationalize, and that simple excuse would pacify me.

I was so worried about us getting caught, because sometimes "we" would. I was her co-defendant, and knew how to lie like a professional when we were apprehended. "Mister, please let us go. You made a mistake" I would plead, charming the undercover store detective with my childish innocence. It would work all the time. Even the store detective that knew she was a regular had felt sorry for me, so they would let her go after lecturing her and threatening to call Children's Services on her if she trespassed again. They loved me, so they never made the call. I was a little ham and would start chatting away, before you knew it, they were laughing and playing with me. They would simply let us go without calling the police. My mother and I both knew the drill, but one time she went too far.

I was five years old when she took me to a popular, drug infested park, which was known for the variety of marijuana, heroin and pills that could be bought or sold there. It was in Manhattan on the lower east side. I remember she used to say, "Toki, we are going to the fourteenth street Park to play." My sister and I would get so excited, because we loved playing on the swings. We would be there all day, but when it got dark, we would be hungry and ready to leave. One particular day, however, she decided to sell her pills. She used to get them from the psychiatric doctors, for her depression, but she made it into another one of her hustles. The psych doctors gave her the good pills like Trazodone and Zanax. That was the last time I saw my mother until I turned seven years old. She was arrested and I was sent to live with my godmother and her husband, Maxwell Robinson (God bless his soul). My baby sister, Raquele, was already living with them. For some strange reason, Rocki never bonded with our mother. As a baby, she would scream uncontrollably, which eventually frayed our mother's nerves and blew her high. It was so bad that our mother gave her to our godparents when she was very young. I was five years old when I joined my sister, who was about two years old by then.

As much love as they lavished upon us, I was still very miserable. I missed my mommy and worried about her. I didn't know that she had been arrested that day at the park for unlawful sales of narcotics. It seemed like she had just disappeared off the face of the earth: no phone calls, no visits, no Mommy. It was very hard on me emotionally. No matter how good my godparents treated me, I would walk around with an attitude; sucking my teeth and stomping my feet. As I grew older, my 'tude didn't improve. I was being raised in a middle-class neighborhood with working-class people, which was a far cry from the drug addicts and thieves my mother had me around, so it was very ungrateful of me to behave like I did.

I hated going to church three times a week, and then all throughout the weekend. My godmother was an elder in the church and the president of the missionary; therefore, she was very active in the church functions. I was force-fed church and rebelled, big time. To make matters worse, we weren't allowed to go outside. That was insane to me! All of my friends would be playing outside and I would have to watch them from the terrace, longing for a chance to play with them. It was not going to happen! Don't get me wrong, it wasn't cruel or intentional punishment. My godmother was just a very paranoid, older woman in her sixties, who loved us so much that she became obsessively over protective. It messed my head up! I just wanted to go outside, but I couldn't understand the reasons for not allowing me the privilege. We lived in a decent neighborhood in the East Flatbush section of Brooklyn; therefore, it was no valid reason for my incarceration. That's exactly how I felt (like I was locked up). So, when I finally got a chance to taste freedom, I took off and running. I promised myself I would never deprive my child of his or her freedom when I give birth to one. It had stunted my growth socially, because I wasn't used to playing outside and interacting with my peers. I actually got teased and taunted for not being able to come outside, and it became a very embarrassing situation. It caused my bitterness to grow and I became very resentful.

My mother came home from prison when I was seven years old. My sister and I would visit her on weekends and summer vacations. Those were my happiest times and I wanted more, because we had so much fun together. I remember simple things like lying in the bed with my mother, watching her favorite soaps, or when she would take turns tickling my sissy and I, until we laughed hysterically and surrendered. She was clean and trying to get her act together and I was proud of her. The poor thing had ruined one of her kidneys with all the drugs in her system at such a young age. She contracted a kidney disease and had to undergo dialysis. It was horrible! She went to the hospital three times a week, hooked up to a dialysis machine, which lasted four hours. She would get attached to all of these tubes that transferred her blood to the artificial kidney to be cleaned and returned to her body. The process was very draining, which caused my mother to become very depressed. This opened up the gates for her addiction to kick back in, but I have to give it to her, she tried to fight it just to be with us. I begged my mother to let me come back and live with her. Also, with some heavy pleading with my godmother, I was allowed to go back. However, my godmother was adamantly against this move, because she knew that my mother's drug habit could possibly return.

So, against her protest, I went back to live with my mother, but my little sister chose to stay behind. I was in my glory until I had a taste of P.S. 67, the public school that was located smack in the middle of the Fort Greene projects. That was where my mother resided, which was the most notorious housing projects in Brooklyn. Those kids were a rough bunch and I definitely did not fit in. I wasn't ready for the transition. The treacherous kids immediately smelled my fear and zeroed in on me. In their eyes, I was a rich kid, because my godfather would bring me lunch every day at lunch time. He would arrive in his station wagon that he used for a cab. Let's just say to a bunch of second graders, his old "Betsy" looked like a limousine.

I was well- spoken and stuck out like a sore thumb with my manners and proper speech, which got me instantly "befriended" by the school bully. She strongly suggested that I bring some money to school and give it to her and her buddies. It was extortion at its best. That's how bad some of those project kids were. I was scared to death and didn't want any problems, so I started stealing my godmother's church money when I would visit her on the weekends. She was the treasurer for the missionary group in her church and I knew where she kept her stash. Not only was I robbing my godmother, I also stole from my mother's boyfriend every chance I got. I obediently handed over the cash to my bully, which was much to her and her cronies delight. They made me feel like I was their best friend, with only the slightest threat when the twenty and fifty-dollar bills slowed up. It was amazing how these young children knew the art of coercion. All I knew was I didn't want to get beat up by the hard core little gangsters.

I almost came close to getting my butt kicked by another tough, little pit bull with red hair. She hated my guts and was jealous, because she couldn't get in on the extortion gig. The other crew had that on lock, so she started harassing me. One day, she waited for me after school, and tried to make me fight her. She and her crew had me surrounded in a circle, taunting me with insults. I will never forget the fear that I felt, and how my heart pounded in my chest. I ran while the whole school chased me, anxious to see me get beat down. I made it to my mother's building and slipped into the pissy smelling elevator before the unruly kids made it into the hallway. When I burst into my apartment, crying hysterically, my mother couldn't believe my story. She began to rant and rave about the situation. At first, I thought the outrage was because those animals were trying to attack her baby. On the contrary, however, she was furious because I didn't fight the bully, and I ran like a chicken. Huh? I couldn't believe it! She actually wanted me to go down stairs and fight the girl. I looked at her like she was an alien with two heads. That wasn't my nature. I wasn't about to go up against those beast. Suddenly, I longed for the peaceful existence I had when I lived in the middle-class neighborhood with my godparents.

Now, I realize my mother was trying to teach me not to be a punk, but I wasn't ready back then. I didn't have enough anger built in me during those times, but it surely reared its ugly head in my later years. Like all things, the party finally ended and the shit hit the fan. My teacher saw me passing forty dollars to my bully. She immediately wanted to know where I had gotten so much money from, and why was I giving it to the girl. The investigation was launched and both my mother and godmother were contacted.

Mrs. Robinson wasn't having it! She immediately had me transferred back to the school district I grew up in. That was the end of my stay with my mother until I turned fourteen years old.

At the age of eight, I began reading adult novels. I just loved to sneak and read my mother's Jackie Collins and Sydney Sheldon books. I was addicted to trashy novels and couldn't get enough. Jackie Collins taught me about the world of the rich and famous, and how they lived with such sexual debauchery and outrageously lavish lifestyles. I wanted that lifestyle! I wanted to blow-up and be a famous celebrity. I didn't have any particular career goal I just knew I wanted to be rich and famous. That was instilled in me from an early age. My money addiction came a few years later, but the seed was planted at eight years old.

Chapter Two

MY LIFE

Back at home with my godmother, I excelled in school, and I was the valedictorian at my junior high school graduation. My favorite teacher, Mr. Nash, referred me to a gifted program for advanced academics, which everybody was excited about. I knew that I was smart, but I didn't consider myself a genius. When I got to high school, I realized that I was actually terrible in math, and the "smart" thing was overrated. I could barely keep up with the Caucasians and Asian students who were wizards in math. I was out of my league. Although I did well in English and Creative writing, I failed miserably in Math and Science, which caused my grades to plummet. I had let my family down and shortly thereafter, I was kicked out of the gifted program. That ruined my desire for school. I started skipping school to hang out with my friends, rather than face the fact that I wasn't able to compete. Peer pressure is real! Instead of applying myself and trying to keep up, I slacked off in school, while opting for new experiences. For one, I picked up a nasty cigarette habit, because I wanted to fit in. I was being a follower: the cool girls smoked, so I wanted to be down. It was a disgusting practice, but I loved blowing smoke rings and acting like I was grown. I managed to kick that nasty habit when I turned nineteen years old. I feared that I was a shoe-in for cancer, since I had a hacking cough from smoking two packs a day, starting at the tender age of fourteen. I believe that it actually stunted my growth, because my mom and dad were both tall in stature, but I have long legs and a short torso! CIGARETTES SUCK!

Then there were the boys. My body had started developing and sex was a hot topic. I, for one, didn't have any legitimate, sexual desires, but since all my friends were "doing it", I wanted to be down. I had just turned fourteen when I lost my virginity at a hooky party thrown down the hall from my apartment. If my godmother would have known that, not only was I skipping school, but I was down the hall having sex, she would have dropped dead. I still remember the boy. He was basically a hook up. I didn't know him personally, but he was a homeboy of my friend's boyfriend. A rather unromantic hook up, I might add. There were absolutely no sparks between us. It was such a casual matter. I told him I wanted to lose my virginity and he grinned like a buffoon, and then climbed on top of me. I felt an uncomfortable poke and a slight burning sensation, and, four humps later, I was indoctrinated into the sex club. The only thing I felt was disappointment. I kept waiting to feel the big deal that all my friends were raving about, but instead, I felt nothing. The entire situation was a waste of my time! I thanked him for "nothing", got dressed, and chilled to three o'clock. That way, I could pretend that I attended school and arrived home.

My real sexual experience happened when I met this cutie outside of my church. I was in the corner store, buying some candy, when this older hunk came up and started to flirt with me. I almost did a double take like... Who, me!? I couldn't believe he was asking me for my number, I looked like a complete dork in my church dress, and he was clearly older than my fourteen years. I found out that he was seventeen years old, which made him seem so cool and mature. Shoo, he was cool and mature. He was a thug, or may be a drug dealer. Who knew? All I cared about was that he liked me. I started calling him and we arranged to meet at his crib. I was floating on cloud nine. I knew that we were going to have sex, and I was going to finally feel what making love felt like. I was in love already, or at least I thought so. He didn't disappoint me! He wasted no time with the small talk and quickly undressed me, which I had no problem with. I was very excited and wanted to experience real sex. First of all, he was thick and had a nice length. It was intimidating at first, but he proved to be quite the considerate lover. He thought I was still a virgin and loved it. I knew enough to know guys loved to feel like they are the first to pop a girl's cherry. I skipped school for a month straight, to go to his house for hours of sex 101 and I excelled in that subject. I became a straight "A" student.

Soon, I was kicked out of the gifted school altogether, and was put into an alternative school for truancy. That was the beginning of my downfall. Fourteen was a coming-of-age time in my life. I've had enough of the strict rules and not being allowed to go outside. I was really "smelling myself" (my godmother's term for being grown) and nobody could tell me nothing. So, I decided it was time to give it another shot with my mother. She was in recovery and hadn't been in jail for a while. It was time for me to be with her again. It was the worst move I have ever made in my life.

In the beginning, it was a great move. My mom and I were best friends, so we had a nice time reuniting and vibing with each other. I was on top of the world. I wasn't the scared, little girl from the middle-class neighborhood any more. I loved the Projects and made plenty of friends from my years of weekend visits. Even my former bullies became cool with me and, unlike my godmother my mother let me go outside. I loved it! Unfortunately, I picked up another nasty habit - boosting. Stealing was in my blood. My mother was a thief and, inadvertently, she taught me the art when I was a little girl. It all came back. Instinctively, it was second nature for me. I thrived in the art of making things disappear on my person, and I became the best at it, which is a sad claim to fame.

I remember the first time I went boosting in A&S department store, which was located downtown on Fulton St in Brooklyn. All the boosters would gather in front of Albee Square Mall, along with the guys who would go to Midtown Manhattan and snatch the money bags from the local merchants when they did their bank drops. It was wild and exciting. Everybody who was somebody in Brooklyn hung out at the Albee Square Mall.

My two best friends and I decided to stop dreaming about Guess jean jumpers and actually go and steal some. I forgot whose idea it was, but I was so with it. We crept into the department store and headed up the escalator to the Guess section. We had no plan, and none of us had ever actually stolen anything before, so we were nervous but determined. We located the denim jumpers and immediately started yanking off the buzzers, recklessly tearing holes in the clothes. My adrenaline was pumping wildly as I wobbled to the exit with the jumper and a Mickey Mouse sweater (they were popular items back then) between my legs, stuffed in my boosting girdle. Two seconds before I reached the door, I burst into a sweat.

I just knew someone was going to grab me. Luckily, I got away with it. That time.

Our noses were wide open. You couldn't tell us anything after that. We tore that department store up! I had every flavor Coco Cola, Mickey Mouse, and Guess Jumper there was. I would say around the tenth boosting spree, the shit hit the fan. By then, my partners and I were cocky. We thought that we could waltz in any store and take whatever we wanted. The undercover store detectives in A&S had a trick for our butts. As we were leaving, they ambushed us. We tried to make a run for it, but as we scattered about, racing to the exit, they tackled us, and then dragged us to the security office. The gig was up! Our parents were contacted and had to come pick us up from the store because of our juvenile status. My home girls were done, but I wasn't deterred in the slightest. I looked at my mother as she tried to lecture me about stealing, saying to myself, "Please! I know she 'aint talking. She taught me how to steal." She just shook her head and called me hard headed. She knew good and well that she passed the disease on to me.

After a while, I got better at stealing, while she felt bad and apologized for stealing in front of me. She admitted to inadvertently teaching me how to become a thief. I felt like I had surpassed the master, because my mother was a petty thief. I, on the other hand, became a professional. I graduated from clothes to high-end merchandise like sable and mink coats, which was a big accomplishment in the underworld.

The first time we got caught, I vowed that I would get better. I was so greedy that I would get caught in Macy's on the 34th Street and 7th Avenue entrance, but they would let me go due to my juvenile status, then I would go right back in the store via the 6th Avenue entrance and start stealing again. It was like a drug and I was hooked. The adrenaline rush I felt when I stole was better than sex. I was insane!

Two months after I moved in with my mother, the worst thing in the world happened to us. She was diagnosed with AIDS. Nothing compares to the devastation of a fourteen year old finding out that her mother was going to die from a horrible disease. My mother had the worst luck in the world. First, she was riddled with illness from the age of seventeen when she found out about her kidney failing. Then, at the age of thirty-four, she was told that she was going to die. Prior to that, she was in and out of the hospital due to complications with her kidneys. So, in retrospect, I can't blame her for getting high. Nothing prepared me for the crack epidemic that hit the 'hood hard in the 80's. Almost all my friends' parents (if the father was around) got high off of crack or heroin. When my mother broke the news to me about her having AIDS, I totally freaked out. At that time, nobody knew anything about that disease, but it was known to kill off its victims very quickly. The disease was so new that the doctors had no idea how to contain or cure the epidemic. I cried hysterically and was almost inconsolable. I had finally reunited with my mother and she was going to die. That was also the end of her recovery. She immediately picked up the crack pipe.

The next day, I came home from boosting to find my mother holed up in her room with about five of her "new" friends. I say that because I had never seen these people before. I knocked on my mother's bedroom door and she wouldn't open it up. Then I smelled a strange, sour, sweet odor wafting in the air. It was the pungent smell of crack. I couldn't believe that my mother was getting high again. She had promised me that she was going to stay clean and be the mother I've always wanted. When she finally opened her bedroom door, she looked like a zombie. That just made it worst, because she was already disfigured from the renal failure. Her skin had darkened and she wasn't attractive any more. I'll never forget how dilated her pupils were, and the glazed, spacey look she had when I accused her of relapsing. She tried to lie but could barely get the words out. She was stuck! At that moment, I knew that I'd lost my mother. It was like a demon had taken over her body. Her eyes looked almost lifeless. My life was never the same after that day. I tried to tell her that we could fight the virus together. Like she was doing with her kidney disease, but she was just too weak in spirit. It was much easier for her to forget her pain and suffering by getting high.

I had never met my father. I had only spoken to him a few times while he was in prison, but I needed him more than ever. Every time he came home from one of his bids, he would promise to come see me, but it never happened. When my mother started on her shit again, I needed him in my life. I didn't want to go back and live with my godmother. I had to take care of my mother, but I really felt alone. I was too young to have all of that stress on me, and I cracked a few times. She started selling all of the furniture in our apartment and stealing from me, which eventually caused me to suffer a breakdown.

I know now that my first attempt at suicide was a ploy to make her stop getting high. I had a nasty argument with my mother after she sold the washing machine and our dining table. I called her every name in the book. At that point, I had lost all respect for her. She had broken another one of her promises to go to rehab, so I threatened to kill myself. I actually climbed out onto the ledge of our eighth floor apartment and refused to come in. Someone called the fire department and they coaxed me down from the ledge. That was my first attempt at suicide. The second time, I took a lethal combination of her medication. I had mixed the AIDS meds with the kidney failure drugs. I told her that since she wanted to kill herself, she should just do it, and then I offered her the pills. Of course, she refused to ingest the lethal dose of medication, so I began to swallow down the pills like a madwomen. I had to get my stomach pumped, and the hospital wanted to send me to a psychiatric hospital for juveniles. I didn't want to go, so I had my mother and my best friend, Queenie, sneak me out of the hospital. It was like "Mission Impossible", but they got me out of there. My mother felt so much guilt that she would do anything for me.

She knew that I was torn up mentally over her problems, but she was too messed up to fix it. I resented her back then, because I felt like all she had to do was stop getting high. It obviously wasn't that easy. I wish that I could tell her that I understand it now, but it's too late. My biggest regret is that I was too hard on her while she was in the midst of her addiction. My life was full of turmoil and pain. The only relief I had was the streets, so I dived head first into crime and deviant behavior. The gifted little girl with the good manners was gone. I was slowly dying and being reborn as Satan's daughter. I lost all faith in God. If there was a God, why was my mother suffering the way she was? That was how I thought, but the reality is that she did it to herself. The years of shooting heroin combined with unprotected sex with her boyfriend, who was also an addict, simply caught up with her. That situation made me very bitter, more than when I longed to be with her as a child. It seemed like I would never be happy.

Chapter Three

DON'T TURN OUT LIKE ME

This is the chapter that I really want my daughter and other young girls in the world to analyze and learn from. I ruined the first part of my life by making all of the wrong choices. I was using my mother's mistakes and her life as an excuse to destroy my own. That was truly sad. I would never want anybody to repeat the mistakes that I made. I hope by telling my story, it will prevent young girls who can relate and dealing with similar situations from wrecking their lives.

I started selling drugs for a local dealer named Kelvin Martin a.k.a. Fifty Cent. He was the gangster from Fort Green projects who the rapper, Curtis

Jackson, named himself after. I had decided to switch up my hustle because I was getting too hot in the stores. I took a shot at selling crack. I hated staying with my mother because of all the drug activity that she brought into our apartment. It became a crack den, and she started stealing from me to feed her addiction. My home had become a living nightmare. I just wanted to make a lot of money and get my own crib. I had dreams of getting rich by selling drugs, but, boy did that turn into a fiasco.

I worked for twenty percent off of every hundred that I made, which was a measly amount for all of the risk that I took. Fifty Cent knew that if I got caught, I wouldn't do anytime due to my juvenile status. My downfall was that I wanted to buy clothes from the crack head boosters and, before I knew it, I had dipped into his cut of the money too many times. I didn't realize it until the shorts began to add up, and he brought it to my attention the hard way. Fifty sent Crime, one of his lieutenants to bring me to meet him. I was very nervous. He had never dealt with me directly, and I was intimidated to meet the infamous gangster. He was known for his ruthlessness, and I didn't know what to expect. I was brought to a building in Farragut Houses, the projects where we sold the drugs, and then escorted to the roof for the meeting. It was all done in silence. I almost shitted my pants when I stood in front of him. It was not his stature, because he was all of fight foot three. He was a little man with a deep growl and, when he spoke, it's almost like he was barking at you "**YO, B***H WHAT UP WITH MY MONEY?**" he barked. I almost collapsed.

"What do you me-mea-mean? I stuttered, shaking uncontrollably. I knew exactly what he meant. My shopping had caught up with me, and I was about to feel it.

"Well since you don't know what I'm talking about, how 'bout I tell you, he stated calmly then roared, "**I WANT MY MOTHERF*****G MONEY, NOW! B***H, YOU BEEN DIPPING AND YOU OWE ME FOUR HUNDRED DOLLARS HOE!**"

"I didn't dip in your money. I swear to god," I cried. I was beginning to hyperventilate. I looked at him and Crime wildly, trying to figure out how I was going to get out of the situation, and wondering why the hell were we having this discussion on the roof.

"**I WANT MY SHIT, B***H! OR YOU 'GONNA HAVE TO SUCK ME AND MY MAN'S D**K RIGHT NOW**" I was horrified at the thought and sick to my stomach. My mind was racing and, all I knew was, I wasn't going to suck nobody's d**k.

"**IT WASN'T ME!!**" I yelled frantically, trying to convince this ruthless, cold-blooded killer that I didn't steal his drug money. I started telling on the other worker, and blaming her for everything. I didn't care! All I knew was I wasn't going down by myself.

'**B***H, IF YOU DON'T COME UP WITH MY LOOT, I'MA THROW YOUR A** OFF THIS F*****G ROOF**" he threatened, his growl as ferocious as a Lion when he attacks his prey.

"I will get you your money. Please don't killllllllllllllll meeeeeee" I started wailing.

"**B***H, SHUT UP! I'M GOING TO MURDA' YOUR ASS IF YOU DON'T GET MY MONEY TO ME BY TOMORROW.**" He dragged me to the edge of the roof, and squeezed my neck, and whispered in my ear, "*Hoe, you better have my money*" then he abruptly released me. Most importantly, he didn't sodomize me, which I was forever grateful for. After telling my mother and my sister's father, who was staying with my mom at the time, what transpired, they both managed to come up with four hundred dollars, so that I wouldn't die. That was one time that my mother put me before getting high. She knew the situation was serious. Plus, with the reputation that Fifty Cent had in the streets, she wasn't going to let her baby get hurt. I loved her for that.

That was the end of my stint as a drug dealer. I never tried that bullshit again. I was utterly traumatized. Ironically, a few months later, I started messing with him. This was not by choice, but by demand. I was visiting my best friend's aunt when in walked my worst nightmare-Fifty Cent. I was in complete shock, and I nearly fainted. I was hoping to never lay eyes on dude again, but there he was, standing in the door way with an evil grin on his face. "Come here, bitch! Long time, no see" he said smirking at me. "Hi, Fifty" I said meekly, hoping he would finish talking to his aunt. I had no idea that she was even related to him. He grabbed my arm and dragged me into the other room like a caveman, and then flung me onto the bed. The unthinkable was taking place and I couldn't believe that his aunt was letting it happen. I mean, if a grown lady couldn't control this madman, I didn't stand a chance in hell. He was around twenty- four and I was a tender fifteen. That was definitely illegal. It was the norm for most of the drug dealers and hustlers in the hood to sleep with underage girls. It was never an issue because most of our mothers were either drug addicts or drunks. So who cared? Plus, no one who I associated with had a father-figure in their home, so we looked for that guidance in the older guys from our 'hood.

From that day on, I became Fifty's girl, which only defined me as being one of the many girls he dealt with. I guess he liked my innocence, because I was definitely not in his league (at that time). I would never allow my fourteen year old daughter, who is eleven at the time of this writing, to date a twenty-four year old man. Mentally, a young girl is just not ready for the mind screwing (manipulation) that an older man can do to her.

That relationship didn't last long. Kelvin Martin a.k.a Fifty Cent became a police informant after he was busted carrying a pistol. He snitched on several dudes in the projects and was hated by many. Shortly after that, he made an attempt to cross the wrong individual and, for that mistake, he was murdered. He was literally gunned down in a stairwell and left to die. That's Street Justice! The eighties were definitely a wild era. It seemed like most of the hustlers in my projects had started to murder each other. I believe the crack epidemic played a huge part in the backstabbing and envy that caused a lot of the murders in Fort Greene. When money comes into play, it becomes a power struggle, and grimey behavior follows suit. The Pony Pack was the most powerful drug organization in my projects at that time, and the majority of the guys involved were either killed or locked up for the rest of their lives. Those who survived death, but lost their freedom, if you're reading this, I urge you to be strong and grateful for your life. Don't ever stop fighting for your liberty, because everybody deserves a second chance. To the few O.G's (Original Gangsters) who made it and survived that era, while maintaining their freedom, I'm sure they are grateful.

The crack had my mother so gone that I would bring grown men into the apartment to sleep with them. I did that to get her attention, but she wouldn't say a word. I got away with murder because she wasn't in her right state of mind. Anyone with an addict for a parent knows that the roles sometimes reverse and the child becomes the responsible care taker of the parent. Also, the child will take advantage of the situation by doing unacceptable things because of the impaired state of the parent. Basically, anything goes, because who cares? When you're getting high, you began to mask your feelings and prevent yourself from being emotionally attached. I know that I've took full advantage of my mother's state of mind. I lost all respect for her and didn't have much left for myself. I was on autopilot for self-destruction. The streets had matured me beyond my years, and I became affiliated with all the popular hustlers in Brooklyn. The gangsters and drug dealers all knew me and my partner, Queenie. We earned reputations for being elite hustlers; not to mention, my reputation for busting my gun (shooting people), which I will elaborate about further in my autobiography.

I was bad beyond belief. I would get caught stealing and never considered stopping. I simply learned from my mistakes. Before I knew it, I had developed quite a rap sheet. Now, years later, I have over 36 convictions for various larcenies and misdemeanors, along with 6 felony convictions for various robberies and assaults. As of this writing, my last criminal conviction was for 65 counts of credit card fraud, which I pleaded down to forgery and unlawful use of credit cards. I was sentenced to five years in prison and served forty-two months. At that time, I was sent to a mother-and-child half way house for six months, where I reunited with my daughter. Altogether, my prison time totals up to thirteen years. I was a hot mess and the epitome of a bad girl, thus the title of my autobiography: **Tales of an Original Bad Girl**. I had decided not to dwell on the details of my scheming and criminal behavior, because I don't want to inadvertently teach people how to hustler. However, I focused on the bad side of the lifestyle, hoping to discourage the would-be copycats in the world from taking the path that I once took in life.

On the flip side, I got away with more than I paid for and managed to live a lavish lifestyle. I'm a survivor who lived my life on my own terms. I have always been a renegade, but now I am happy to finally have order in my life. I don't have to look over my shoulder and wonder if I will make it to the exit of a store without being apprehended.

After doing my last five year bid, I reunited with my daughter, and I was ecstatic! I can't put into words how happy I was to be with my baby girl again. She was all I thought about while I was away. I'm so blessed that my best friend Queenie, who is also her godmother, raised my daughter in my absence. Queenie gave my baby the life that she deserved. My ex-husband had wanted custody of her, but I felt it would be better for her to live with her godparents who had more to offer. She lived in a beautiful home in Ohio, and enjoyed a great life while I was gone.

My ex-husband, on the other hand, lived with his mother in the projects, and thought that he could provide our child with the lifestyle that she was used to. He meant well, but I had to make a judgment call. With the hate and contempt that he felt for me, he would have surely turned my baby against me. The first two years of my incarceration, my daughter thought that I was on tour, and everything that her godmother bought her, she thought it came from me. She told her grand stories of me being a big star, and how I had to travel and perform all over the world to make money to take care of her. Whatever she gave her son, she gave my daughter, and those children were lavished upon. She even told my daughter that her father worked hard to send her money, and how he loved her so much that we would fight over who loved her the most. I thought that was generous of her, because, in reality, he didn't send her any money to help with her care. Nor did he send me anything after all I had done for him, before, during, and after his eleven year bid. I basically dropped out of school, following him around from city to city, while he was on the run for murder. I stood by him during his incarceration. I even married him in prison, making it possible for him to have conjugal visits, and that was the thanks I got. Wow! Those are some of the reasons I can't trust a man with my heart. I know this is a random thought, and I'm straying away from the topic, but I had to get that out of my system. I promise I will get back to my childhood.

My best friend instilled positive stories inside of my daughter to keep my memory alive for the years that I was gone and, also, to keep the existence of her father in perspective. I wouldn't allow him to see her while I was gone because he wanted custody of her badly. The police told him that if he could get her in his possession, that her godmother had no legal rights to guardianship. I struggled with that decision, but I knew that Velvet would be raised better with Queenie. He would have had her calling some other lady "mommy" and that would have destroyed me.

I tell my daughter as much about my life as I feel that she can handle. I always tell her 'Don't turn out like me'. I wrote a song about it, and I hope it can be an anthem for all the hustlers (active and retired). The song lets the children know that whatever they may have done in life, it's not the right thing to do, and how much more their parents want for them. I always say, 'I did it all, so that my baby won't have to do it'. When I was in the halfway house, I was selected to speak to the troubled at-risk teens in various schools, and I loved it. Public speaking is natural for me because I am a performer. I loved to tell my story, while hoping to prevent young children from choosing the path I did.

The gangs of today remind me of the different crews I used to run with. We ran to the streets because of different family issues. Most of us had addicts as parents; therefore, we found love and guidance from the misguided youths that we've met in the underworld. It is an advanced form of peer pressure, which is easy for one to fall victim to its influence. The allure of street life, violence and crime is like the ultimate drug. It's twice as addictive, but the side effects and repercussions are lethal. The havoc it wreaks on your life is irreversible, because once you catch a case, that's a mark on your life. Society views felons and ex-cons as being the scum of the earth. Period! The worst feeling is standing before a judge as he flicks through the various pages of my lengthy rap sheet. He glances at me in disgust, and silently forms his opinion of me from the hideous charges he has read. My life is summed up in a thick file that is called my Arrest Jacket. The definition of a jacket is an article of clothing that covers your person. My Arrest

Jacket covers my life of crime. I just want to rip it off and shed myself of that negative image. I despise what I appear to be on paper. I pray that all the youth, those that are caught up in the addiction of street life, make it out before it's too late. If not, they will end up wearing the jacket of shame for the rest of their lives. Just like I do! My only chance of peeling off a layer of that jacket is to make a success out of my life. With the help of this book, along with, my music, I can turn my sob story into a successful ending. Then I can say to my daughter that I've changed and made something of myself. I am an Entrepreneur. If I can do it, so can anyone else who desires to change. Do things differently and get different results. Don't turn out like me. Turn out better!

My Mother
at 16 yrs old

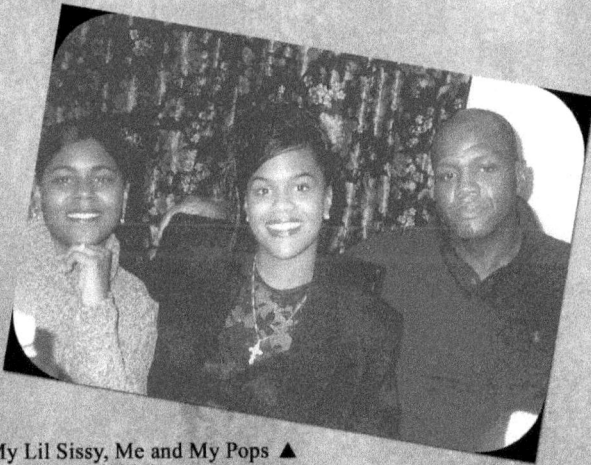

My Lil Sissy, Me and My Pops ▲
(1996)

Velvet 2 Years Old
Sucking Her Finger Sideways
Like My Mom Did. It Gave Me Chills!
I Know My Mom Lives Through Her

Lil MackMama
2 Years Old

▲ Young Natoka
14 Years Old
At My Mom's Crib
in Forte Green
Before The Crack Made Her
Sell All The Appliances..Damn!

▲ 14 years old
Fly Girl

Visiting my Then-Husband
Secret Squirrel
a.k.a Victor L.Washington
18 Years Old ▼

▼   Future MackMama

Gee from P.A.
Me (15 Years Old)
▼ My First Mink Coat

"VICTOR + MATOKA"
FOREVER. IN LOVE !!
UNTIL WE KISS AGAIN

▲ 15 Years old.
Young and In Love

Me at 15. I Loved Rocking Silk Suits
and Gucci Bags.
▼ I was in My Apartment in Forte Green

▲ Throwback
My Homie on the Left
I Forgot his Name...oops.
Me and Hawk (right)
16 Years Old

▲ Me at 14 Years Old

Me, Gee, Poppi, Vikki ▲
Me at 14 Years Old
(Too Damn Grown ... lol)

My Sister and Angie Came To
Visit Me in
▼ Bayview Correction Facility 1993 ▼

▲ You Know This is a Throwback
From The 90's
I Was Rocking
A Jean Shirt with a
Jean Prairie Skirt....lol

◄ The Sexy 20's

◄ Me and
My Horsie
(4 Years Old)

My GodMother
Louise A.Robinson
(R.I.P.)
Maxine and Me
26 Years Old ►

◄ My Nana
Janie Williams
and Me
(at 26 Years Old)

My God Parents
and Lil Jonette
▶

◀ Me at
7 Months Pregnant
and
My God Sister
Jonette

My Homeboy Karief and Me
14 Years Old ▶

Big Kisha, Tawana (Grimey)
Tracy, Natoka 17 Years Old
Throwback

Understanding aka Undeas
Inside Uncle Benny's Spot
on Fulton St. ▼

▲ The Day I Met My Pops
Bayview Corr FacilityVisit
19 Years Old

Velvet 1st Birthday
Queenie and My Godson T.J.
(2002) ▲

◄ Rob (R.I.P.)
My Sister's First Love
(1994)

▲ Killer Ben '87

Tracy Washington ▲
and Universal

▲
King Tut and Red Bug

Free
Sherm "The Worm" ▲

▲ Jamel "Ja" Norris (R.I.P.)

▲
(Top Row) Itru, Bar, J-Rock, Rap, Jamel, Supreme Magnetic
and G-Man (Middle Row) Lamel, Baby Rock
THE INFAMOUS PONY PACK
from Forte Green Projects (1986)

B. Original ▶

◀ Shaquell and BooLay

JuJu (1986) ▶

Chapter Four

What You 'Gonna Do?

The first person I shot was this guy from Farragut projects, located a few blocks away from Fort Greene. The incident happened out of desperation, a sort of kill or be killed situation. It took place when I was only fifteen years old. I was messing around with my childhood love and ex-husband, whose nickname is Secret Squirrel. At the time, he was on the run for a body (murder), we were like a modern day Bonnie and Clyde. However, he was insanely jealous. He would sniff cocaine and hallucinate about me cheating on him. This one particular time, I sold some clothes to this guy from his projects, but the asshole lied on me. He went back and told Squirrel's sister that he was screwing me, and I gave him the clothes for free. All hell broke loose when that lie got back to Squirrel. He was so sneaky that I never saw it coming. That's why his nickname is Secret Squirrel.

"Eh, Toka, what you did today?" he questioned casually as we were lying naked on the couch after making love. My mother was in the hospital, so I had the crib to myself.

I had been dating Squirrel for a few months and was head over heels for him. He had a "baby mother" and with that came a lot of drama, but I was his ride or die chick and proud of it. He was twenty four and had me, a fifteen year old, running around with him while he was on the lamb from the police. He was even featured on America's Most Wanted. I was loyal to a fault and looked up to this man like he was my father. I even went so far as to call him "Daddy". That's what happens when you don't have your father in your life, you look for that father figure in a man.

I answered his question. I told him that I sold some gear to the dude, but before I could finish the story, he jumped up and began to beat me wildly. I was flabbergasted! I could only curl up in a tight ball, while he pummeled my back and rib cage with blows. I was so confused, because although it wasn't his first time beating me up, I didn't have a clue as to what I did to cause his fury. He finally told me the reason when he got tired of assaulting me. He had me pinned on the floor, bruised and battered, as he berated me. "**YOU F*****G WHORE! YOU F****D THAT NICCA!!**" he roared furiously. I couldn't believe that he thought I had sex with my customer until he told me what the liar had said to his sister. I was in disbelief as to why would anybody lie like that for no reason at all.

It just didn't make sense. I denied it vehemently, but it was to no avail. He simply threatened to kill me. I knew that I was dealing with a stone cold murderer, so I didn't take his threat lightly. Drastic measures had to be taken. At that moment, I made up my mind that I was going to shoot the liar and prove my innocence. If I went through such extreme measures, I felt that he would believe me.

The next day, I dressed in all black and borrowed a gun from Squirrel's younger brother, Tracy. He didn't bother to talk me out of my plan. He provided me with the pistol and wished me luck. He warned me not to lose his gun in the process. The gangster mentality in the hood was serious! We were teenagers discussing the probability of hurting someone as casually as asking for the time. That was the underworld I lived in, and the beast I had become.

I devised a master plan to get the liar, whose name is Larrel, to meet me in City Park. That park was the gateway between Farragut and Fort Greene. Everyone walked through there to get back and forth between the two projects. He had no idea that I knew about the vicious lie he spread on me, so I used that to my advantage and rocked him to sleep. He was so excited to meet with me, and probably thought I wanted to really get with him. He had no clue about what I was planning to do to him. It was around 11:00 p.m. --booty call time-- and it was pitch black in the park. I had told him to meet me by the pool entrance at 11:30 p.m., which was a remote, isolated area. Arriving early, I laid in the cut until I saw his tall, lean frame approaching rapidly. I wasn't nervous. Instead, I was furious and wanted justice served. He had to be taught a lesson because that lie could have been fatal to me. Plus, the beating I took behind that charade had caused me so much pain. My back was aching, and I feared that it was dislocated. It was now time for Liar to feel some pain too. My adrenaline was pumping and, when he was directly in front of me, I pulled out the gun on him, which caused him to freeze in his tracks and wipe the dopey grin off of his face. "Yeah 'nicca you lied on me. You thought I was 'gonna let you skate with that shit?" I snarled, pointing the pistol steadily at a spot in the center of his stomach. He was tall and his reflexes went into action instantly as he tried to knock the gun out of my hand. He caught me off guard, but I held on to that 'banga (gun) for dear life until he finally let go and took off running. I started letting off shots **POW...POW...POW.** The third one hit the target. I saw him buckle and grab his leg, but he kept running all the way back to Farragut. I was amped up and excited.

The rush I felt was better than any drug I had ever tried. I felt powerful! I fought back!! I wished that, I had enough courage to shoot Squirrel, but my love for him was too strong. It overpowered the hate that I felt when he beat me. I know exactly how battered women feel when they stay loyal to their abusers and don't leave. It is part of the mental control that they instill in you; the fear and sadly the love that keeps you around for more, hoping that every beating is the last. You want so badly to believe the apologies and cries of love, but it's hard for the abuser to love you if he can't love himself. It is all a horrible sickness on the abuser's part and the victim.

After that incident, I felt invincible. For every beating I took from Squirrel, I bottled that anger up, and let it loose on anyone who violated me. That combined with the resentment I felt about my mother's situation had turned me into a cold callous individual. I didn't care about hurting anyone else, because I was hardened by the continuous beatings that I had to endure. Getting hurt was a normal occurrence. When Squirrel heard about the shooting, he didn't know how to take it. His first reaction was, "You better not try that shit with me, b***h!" that statement was followed by, "Your little ass got heart. That's why I f**k with you." I took it as a proud owner of a pit bull who had just killed another pit bull and her owner rewarded her, but never let the b***h forget who was the master.

My second shooting was after my mother's death. Sadly, she died when I was sixteen from the AIDS virus. It was also the year that I did my first extensive bid, which was twelve months in Nassau County Jail. I was in and out of Juvie (juvenile detention) and graduated to Rikers Island for thirty days here and there, but the biggie was that Nassau County bid. It came thirty days after my mother was buried. I did eight months out of that year and came home a better criminal.

I will never forget how I felt that very first time in the back seat of a police cruiser, handcuffed like an animal. At that moment, you swear to God that you've learned your lesson, and you pray to get out of that predicament. But as soon as you're released, you forget the degrading feeling of being caged like an animal. Before you know it, you're back at it like nothing ever happened. Prison was like college. I learned how to do more crime and excel at them. I was schooled by the old-timers and soaked up all the criminology I could in those eight months. When I was released, I resumed boosting and started recruiting younger girls between thirteen and fourteen years old to be my bag ups.

The term "bag ups" meant that I took them into the stores and loaded up bags and stuffed their girdles, using them as mules to carry the stolen goods out of the stores for me. These girls were wayward street urchins who were wasting away in the streets with no direction. They had no way to get money without degrading themselves by using sex, so Queenie and I took them under our wings. We taught them the game and showed them how to get money. It perpetuated the destruction of their lives, but in our minds, we were helping them and showing them a better life. That was one of the many examples, of my twisted thinking at that time in my life.

The day of the shooting, I was defending one of our bag ups. We pulled up on this girl and her boyfriend, the girl was a hater and was talking shit about us, so we gave the orders and sent our girl to jump out and beat her up. While they were fighting, the boyfriend decides to jump in and punch our girl in the face, giving her a black eye. The situation got crazy! I jumped out of the car and shot him in the stomach, and then we fled the scene. It was a point that had to be made and, that point was, we were not to be played with. We could have easily driven off with our girl's eye blackened, but our reputations were at stake. Drastic measures had to be taken. The boyfriend survived, and so did the guy I shot in the leg prior to that incident; therefore, I wasn't concerned or the slight bit bothered about the repercussions of my actions. I didn't realize that I was doing anything wrong. It was the way of life in my world, and only the strong survived. Violence was par for the course. My philosophy was simple: If any one violated me, I was going to get them back. The slightest infraction was enough to feel my wrath. If you talked about me or my people, or if you did anything to harm me or mines in any manner, it was death before dishonor, and that included a traitor in my crew. We were on that gangster tip hard! That was the birth of O.B.G's (Original Bad Girls). I came up with the name years later when I started rapping, but the concept and the life I lived gave birth to the movement.

My third shooting was based on revenge. The victim was a female I will call her Grimey. She was from Lafayette Gardens, which was another notorious Projects in Brooklyn. She was a booster with a reputation for being a "grimey" chick. I should have stayed clear of her, but all of the hustlers in my 'hood eventually cliqued up and "took" money together.

We began to hang tough, getting money together and smoking dust. I was warned repeatedly about how sneaky and foul this girl was, but I paid it nooch. I felt like we were cool, so she wouldn't get me. I learned from Grimey never to underestimate any one. She was a fly-girl, but one of those types who wanted it all for herself. She was a control freak, and wasn't satisfied unless she had it all. I remember one night I had a sleep over, and I invited her and a couple of girls from her crew over. We had a fun night, but the next day my Polo jacket was missing out of my closet. Back then, Ralph Lauren's Polo design was a big deal, and the pieces were coveted. All of the boosters from different cliques tried to out boost each other, and the LG girls were very competitive and known for being conniving. I knew they had struck when I discovered my jacket missing. I took a loss that day, but vowed to never make the mistake of bringing wolves to my den again.

Stupidly, I didn't stick to that vow and a couple of days later we went on a boosting spree. We descended on the stores in the city like a flock of rabid pit bulls. We took anything we wanted with no regard for the law. That day, she convinced me to leave my burner (pistol) at home. I always carried a gun on me (just in case). I was so wild that I wasn't above pulling my gun out and backing down a security guard to prevent getting arrested. There were times when I had to mace the security to get out of stores. Not to omit, the wild fights I had with security who tried to apprehend me.

So, against my better judgment, I left it home and went out. After a good day, the rental was packed with garbage bags full of stolen merchandise. We ran in and out of the high-end stores in Manhattan until we had accumulated enough merchandise to sell and make money. After our boosting spree, we headed back to Cypress Hill Projects where Grimey had a customer waiting to buy our goods. She told me to come with her into a building in the projects because one of her customers had supposedly wanted to buy all of our merchandise. We got into the elevator rode up several floors. When we finally reached the floor, the door swung open and a guy with the biggest gun I had ever saw stood there in his house slippers. He pointed it directly at me and told me to "run my shit" (give him my jewelry). Now come on! What stick up kid ran around in his slippers robbing people? He looked at me and went directly for my chain and bracelets. I managed to conceal a few of my gold bangles, but he was deliberate about what he wanted from me. He didn't bother to take anything from Grimey, which was a mistake, because it made the whole set up and jack (robbery) obvious.

I was fuming and wanted to f**k her up, but I held my composure until we got down the stairs. I wasn't a fool, and I didn't want to get shot. Once we got downstairs and back into the car, I couldn't believe how nonchalant and unbelievable she was acting after the robbery. I decided to keep my cool and plotted on my revenge. She had her bag ups with her and I didn't have my burner. I didn't want to get jumped on top of the robbery. I knew one thing for certain: I was going to get 'dat bitch! Her griminess kicked in overdrive. That and her greed caused her to have me set up and robbed. She had wanted my jewelry and stopped at nothing to get it. Grimey had violated me in the worst way. She could have gotten me murdered! I've never had anyone set up. If I wanted something, I took it straight up. Never would I smile in your face and stab you in the back, but everyone didn't have morals and principles. There was no honor among thieves!

I got locked up out of town in Pennsylvania the next day; therefore, I had to wait to get at her. I got stuck in Juvenile lock up, waiting for Queenie to come and get me. She had to locate my mother and bring her to the facility to get me out. My mother couldn't stop getting high long enough to come and get me out of my frequent scrapes, so Queenie had to bribe her with crack just to get her to cooperate. Mommy was deteriorating fast and really going hard with the drugs. She was on a death mission and knew that she was dying, so she wanted to go out on her terms.

When I came home, Grimey was actually wearing my jewelry that was taken in the robbery. She was very comfortable, and didn't care if I found out. I guess she thought I was a joke, but I would have the last laugh. My homeboy, Jamel, who was down with the infamous Pony Pack, the notorious crew from Fort Greene, told me that she was "rockin' my jewels" (wearing my jewelry). He was messing with her at the time, but still "put me on" (told me). Her foulness irritated him, and he gave me permission to get her ass. I loved Ja for that. He really had my back. The angel dust had her tripping and thinking she was invincible, but I was going to show her that she wasn't.

I woke up early and took a cab to her aunt's house in Clinton Hills, a section that was originally a part of Fort Greene. I sat patiently on the stoop across the street, waiting for her to come outside and go into her trunk. She lived out of her trunk and slept from place to place; therefore, it was easy to clock her routine. Just as I expected, she came outside around twelve o'clock and headed for her trunk, and began pulling out clothes that she planned to wear for the day. When you hang with a person it's easy to stalk them because, they never switch up their routine. I slipped across the street and walked up behind her. "Eh Grimey, I want my shit," I said calmly. She was so confident and unfazed she didn't even flinch. My attention wasn't to alarm her, and I really didn't want to have to shoot her. I simply wanted my jewelry back. "What you talking 'bout, Ma-to-ka?" she drawled, pronouncing every syllable in my name. The dust made her a space cadet. Everyone always mispronounced my name with an "M" instead of an "N" and I didn't bother to correct them. I was named after a girl with the name Matoka. She was another booster from Fort Greene, who later started getting high, and it caused people to mix up our names. I looked at the lying broad in disgust and wanted to blast her right then and there, but I knew that I couldn't get away with it on foot. I was so furious that I took a cab over and didn't rent a getaway car. At seventeen, I was a professional at putting hits together. I was taught well by my ex-husband.

He was apprehended for his murder charge when he tried to visit me in Nassau County Jail. I thought it was the most romantic thing ever. He had risked his freedom to bring me cosmetics and underwear. I was riddled with guilt because I felt like it was my fault that he got "knocked" (arrested). When I came home, I married him on Riker's Island so that we could have trailer visits, and because I was madly in love with that man; even though he abused me mentally and physically. I now realize that he manipulated me, and made me feel like it was my fault that he went to jail. That way, I would feel obligated to stick with him during his bid. He knew damn well that he could have sent my care package, and he shouldn't have risked his freedom. He was too smart to make such a risky, foolish move. He simply knew it would be hard to continue to run without me supporting him while he was on the lamb. He was a manipulator and had my young mind twisted.

Anyway, I calmed down and used my good ole' "rocking their ass to sleep method" that Squirrel had taught me. I asked the fool to drop me off and she actually said yes. I couldn't believe that she trusted me to sit behind her. It was her cockiness that caused me to lose it. As soon as she pulled up in front of my building, I didn't even wait for her foot to leave the gas pedal before I leaned over and shot her in the thigh with my .38 special. The shits and giggles were over. Her best friend at the time, Tracy, was in the passenger seat, and she gagged. She was wearing Grimey's jewelry and I told her to run it. She started to procrastinate, so I let off another shot to scare her.

POW!! The gunshot echoed in the car and hit the floor in the back seat. She began peeling off the jewels immediately. Grimey was very quiet or possibly in shock. She just kept mumbling over and over, "You shot me!" I responded, "Yeah, b***h, you lucky I didn't kill you. All I wanted was my shit back." I then exited the car, tucked the pistol in the small of my back, and strutted off. It was like a movie. It was broad daylight and everyone heard the two shots and wondered what happened. I became a street legend right then and there. People still talk about that incident.

The fourth victim was personal because she was my girlfriend. Her name is "Goldie". We were very passionate but we fought like lions. I was bisexual from the age of fifteen. An exotic dancer who lived in my mother's building turned me out. At that time, being bisexual or a lesbian was very taboo, so I kept it to myself. But when I met Goldie, I was already "out". We met in prison when I was incarcerated in Rose M. Singer, the woman's detention center on Rikers Island. The Island is huge and detained a great amount of criminals in New York City. My husband was incarcerated and I wanted to remain loyal to him in terms of messing with a man, but as far as I was concerned, getting it on with girls wasn't considered cheating. I couldn't stand Goldie when we first met. She worked in the gym and, also, took pictures for special events. I took some pictures and wanted an extra one. When I attempted to steal the extra picture, she peeped the move, and told me to put it back. I cursed her out and called her a "police". From that day, I despised her in a major way. After I got sentenced, I was transferred to Taconic Correctional Facility, where I bumped into her again. I was surrounded by monsters (ugly chicks) and weighed my options. Did I want to spend my bid by myself, or did I want to mess with someone to make my time go faster? I decided that I wanted a girl, but my choices were very limited until I spotted Pumpkin (Goldie's nickname at the time). I didn't like her cocky attitude, but she was a cutie. I decided to let go of my grudge. I sent my homegirl, Robin, to tell Goldie that I liked her. Goldie immediately told Robin that she liked me, too. It was simple and to the point. We were together the entire bid. Even after Goldie went home, she still kept it real with me, and looked out. She wrote me constantly, and sent me money. We eventually broke up after I started messing with another girl, but we remained friends.

Years later, we reunited in the streets and got back together. She had a job and sold drugs on the side, but I introduced her to my hustle, which was credit card fraud. I had stepped my game up and was making a lot of money. We were not only lovers but partners in crime. She treated me like royalty and loved me unconditionally. However, she had a nasty little secret: she smoked "woolies" (crack mixed in marijuana). I found out when she kept disappearing with my brand new BMW. I thought she was cheating, but she was getting high, and didn't want to come around me. I lost so much respect for her, and I started hitting her. I cheated on her and she used that as an excuse to get high. I thought that was bullshit, and had no understanding to it. She never stole anything from me, and she always kept money, so it wasn't a major problem. But I went through so much with my mother over drugs that I had zero tolerance for the addiction.

My disappointment with Goldie, mixed with the rage built inside of me from the abuse I took from my husband, made me lose it. I used to hit her all the time, and she never hit me back. She would try to subdue me, and that would make it worst. That night, I caused her to lose it, because I blew a kiss at my ex girl. She was furious and literally chased me around my car on 125 Street in Harlem. We fought from Harlem to Brooklyn. It was comical as I recall how we blocked the entrance to the Jackie Robinson Parkway (formally known as the Interboro), while we fought in the car like two maniacs. I was furious! She had me in a headlock while banging me in the head with her cell phone. She had snapped. I knew right then and there that when we got to Brooklyn, I was going to shoot the shit out of her. Of course, I rocked her to sleep and called a truce when we got off the parkway. She was so relieved when I suggested that we go get something to eat and have some drinks. She had completely dropped her guard. A mistake she would live to regret.

I played it cool at the restaurant, telling her that I was sorry, but when we pulled into my garage parking space, I retrieved a gun from one of my stashes and it got ugly. She was a little loose off the Fuzzy Navels she had been downing at the restaurant, and I was determined to teach her a lesson. She was never going to put her hands on me again. The years of abuse that I put up with from my husband was all I was going to deal with ever again. I was so destroyed mentally that I thought it was acceptable to hit her, but was outraged when she finally hit me back.

"Tok, what 'chu doing? Stop playing, man. Chill out, bae" she shrieked nervously when she saw the gun I had in my hand, pointed at her.

"Oh, b***h, you thought it was over, huh?" I taunted her. She ran around the garage, ducking and dodging me, until she managed to escape when another car drove in. I chased her to our building and ran inside the lobby after her. I was on her heels until I got the perfect leg shot. **POW!** I caught her. She yelped and buckled. "**OH SHHHIT! YOU CRAZY, B***H! YOU SHOT MEEE!!**"She yelled in astonishment. The entire block was looking at us in disbelief. Back then, I didn't care who was around. If I was after revenge, I was going to get it. Simple as that! That's how ignorant I was. I had my godsister, Jonette, bring me down some towels. Then I kindly drove her to the hospital and prepared a believable story for the cops. When you come into the ER with a gunshot wound, you better have a good explanation of how you got shot or you may get cuffed. I made her tell the cops that she was robbed and assaulted.

Goldie forgave me, because she knew that I was traumatized from being a battered woman. For one, the worst thing you could possibly do is hit someone who has been abused. It's a good chance they may have a flash back and "go ham on you" (beat you up). The reason why this chapter is called "What You Gonna' Do?" is because the song on the soundtrack is about me having fictitious shoot-outs and getting shot. So, I thought this would be the perfect chapter to tell my readers about my violent situations. It is not to glorify it, but simply to tell the story of my life as hardcore as it was. It made me who I am today.

I often wonder how I escaped being shot or killed. Then I realized that God gave me two angels: my mother and my godmother. That's why he took them away early. He gave them their wings to protect my crazy behind and, surprisingly, I only went to jail for the shooting of Grimey. Irregardless of her foulness, she had the audacity to tell on me. I got that case ran concurrent with the robbery and assault charge that I did four-and-a-half years on. I will tell you about that in another chapter. On a different note, I actually shot and killed a brand new BMW. That was the last time I bust my gun, which was in 2005. My intention was to shoot out the windows, but I was on a ledge, looking over the vehicle. I aimed for the windshield, but I missed and shot the engine instead. I tore that engine up with about five shots. I can't recall the caliber of pistol I used, but it did a lot of damage. That car belonged to a Nigerian guy who I was dating. He was supposed to get my five carat-diamond choker out of the pawn shop but he reneged.

I had pawned it when I was strapped for cash. At that time, my choice of hustle was slow; therefore, I wasn't making any money. It was my most prize possession, and I didn't want to lose it. The Nigerian used to give me credit cards to work, and he was very corrupt. He had his hand into almost everything, which most Nigerians did. They were either, very successful doctors, lawyers or diplomats, but some of them were very successful Crooks. Whatever the case, they all love money, and they knew how to make lots of it.

This guy was very well-dressed and wore the finest Italian wear. He had recently purchased the BMW convertible. It was a brand new coupe, and it still had the temporary plates. He didn't even have insurance on the eighty-thousand dollar vehicle. I didn't like his arrogance, but I dealt with it because he had money. I knew I needed him to give me the three grand that was necessary to get my diamond choker out of the pawn shop. He loved my music and really liked the idea that he was dating an entertainer. That's why I really believed that he was going to give me the money, even though I held out on the sex. My philosophy was 'Hold out till he pays out!' He was not going to get any of my "Nelly"(vagina) until he got my chain out. After that, I was still going to make him wait. Actually, I couldn't stomach him, because he had a bad case of B.O (body odor) as if he didn't really wash. He sprayed on expensive cologne and called it a day. Disgusting!

Three days before the deadline to get my jewelry out, I spent the night with him and he begged me for some nelly. This went on all night and I kept telling him no. He said he just wanted to taste me, and that would satisfy him, so I foolishly gave in. It was the worst head that I had ever received in my life. Then he begged me to give him oral sex. That was going too damn far! I adamantly refused that request, but he wanted it so bad he was almost crying. I started thinking about my diamond choker and made a decision based on desperation. I did it! That bastard violated me and exploded in my mouth. I had never felt so degraded and filthy in my life. I was so mad! I cursed him out, and told him to have my shit out of that pawn shop by the next day. I knew that he did that on purpose. I had made him beg and he wanted to show me who was the boss. It was a belittling tactic to bring me down off of my high horse. It definitely worked! I left his house feeling like a piece of shit. Even though I didn't sleep with him, I still allowed him defile me. Then he violated me on top of that by ejaculating his disgusting sperm into my mouth. I tried to cheer up by thinking about my beloved diamond choker, but I was very antsy, and wanted my money. He told me he would have it for me the next day.

The next day came and I didn't hear a word from him. I called his phone all day, but I only got his machine. He never did that with me, I couldn't stop him from calling my phone and now all of a sudden I couldn't reach him. That fool was trying to play me and my blood started to boil. The deadline to get my diamond choker came and went, but I still I didn't hear from him. I had lost my beautiful diamond choker for good and I saw blood. I went to his complex and sat for hours, waiting for him to come outside, but he was holed up in his crib. He was probably with another chick, which didn't bother me. I just wanted his head on a platter. I was literally pacing back in forth with the gun in my hand until I couldn't take it anymore. That's when I started firing at his car. It was like the fourth of July in his parking lot. I wouldn't stop firing until my gun jammed. I wanted him to come outside so bad, but he didn't even respond to the commotion. He must have been knee-deep in some sex. One thing is for sure, he will never disrespect another American girl like that again. I drove off satisfied with the bullet holes that his precious car was riddled with. I was a little disappointed when I didn't hit the windshield, because I knew how costly it was to replace those on luxury vehicles. At that point, I had no idea that I murdered his engine. Oops! A few hours later, he started blowing up my phone. I picked up casually and said "Hello?"

"What did you do to my 'cur? You crazy b***h?"

"Excuse me? What are you talking about?" I played dumb.

"I know you did it. The security cameras saw you, and there are witnesses. You are going DOWN!" He roared.

I continued to deny it and played dumb. "But I haven't heard from you. Why would I do that?" I feigned innocence, combined with a hint of sarcasm.

"YOU ARE GOING TO JAIL B*H! I WILL SEE TO IT"** he yelled the threat, which I wasn't expecting. He did too much dirt to want to involve the authorities, but the idle threat had me shook. I called Queenie and suggested that she call him. She was able to speak to him in the Nigerian dialect because she was also from Nigeria. She told him to calm down and don't even think about talking to the police. He told her he wasn't going to press charges, but he had something better for me. He had my picture and some of my hair from when I spent the night at his apartment. He threatened to put "roots" on me; otherwise known as a voodoo spell. He told her he was going to send my Cd and picture to Africa, and he would fix me good. I laughed it off and paid him no mind until about a month later. I got locked up for sixty five counts of credit card fraud. I was sentenced to five years. To this day, I believe that he had a voodoo spell put on me, because that amount of time for a non- violent crime like credit card fraud was insane.

I rebuke that devil in the name of Jesus. I pray every day that I don't have any negative spirits on me that will hinder my life. I regret that whole incident because I don't need any bad luck. He told Queenie that his entire engine was destroyed, and he didn't even have insurance. He was on his way down south, where the insurance was cheaper; however, due to my actions, he was not going to be covered. He would have to pay out of pocket to replace his engine. I couldn't have cared less. I wanted him to feel the pain and loss I felt over my precious diamond choker.

I was truly a madwoman. I would always start off cool, but when somebody crossed me with the slightest infraction I would flip out. I am so happy that I have controlled my anger with the help of Anger Management groups in prison. I learned how to think about the consequences of my actions, and several techniques to control my fury. It took me a lot of years, but I finally got my anger issue under control. As much as I hate to admit it, the last prison stint I did really helped me mature into a sensible person, because I was way too cocky and combative. For instance, I had a verbal altercation with the rap artist Remy Martin, who is currently incarcerated with 8 years for shooting her friend over some stolen funds. That situation made me realize that I could have been the one shot. Or I could have shot her and been in a worst predicament. With my criminal record, I would have got hit with eighteen years instead of the eight years she received. I was tripping because she didn't want to give me a verse on my O.B.G's The Movement mixtape (cd).

I was so excited about bringing a collection of hot female emcees together on one mixtape. That would have been great for hip-hop. To have an artist as talented as Remy was big to me and I needed her to be a part of my project. I was a big fan of hers and respected her 'gangsta. I met her at K Slay's album release party in the bathroom. I took the opportunity to introduce myself, and pitch my project to her. She seemed to love the idea of various female emcees coming together to form a super group on my mixtape. She gave me her personal phone number and told me that she would do it. I was so happy, and it made me love her more. She just seemed so real and down-to-earth. This was before her album was released. She was on the verge of major success, but not quite there yet. Imagine my surprise when, a few days later, I called her to set up studio time, and she didn't return my call. I hit her up two more times, but she had her assistant give me the runaround. I am not into kissing ass or begging people for their time. I got the hint that she didn't want to be bothered and left it alone. I was tight because she had me under the impression that she was down.

I flipped and started to diss her at my shows and on my mixtapes. I was in rare Mack Murder form. The saying, 'It's a thin line between love and hate' is a true statement. It's one of Satan's biggest tricks; the ability to make people flip those emotions so easily. I admired Remy so much, but as soon as I got mad, I turned on her. That was definitely wrong. Instead of me thinking about her schedule or what she may have had on her plate with trying to get her album together- I immediately started my 'stinkin thinking. I came to the irrational conclusion that she was a hater and personally dissing me. Therefore she became my primary enemy. (Smh at myself and my behavior- typical street mentality)

I didn't like the one female at a time practice of the music industry. There are a thousand male artist who collaborate, and they have no problem with breaking bread together. But why was it a one at a time system when it came to the females. The only way to change that attitude is through sisterhood in the business. I would like to see at least ten female emcees, simultaneously, climbing the charts, and being played in rotation on the radio. Female emcees are like endangered species in the game, and that is a shame. I was passionate about my O.B.G's and if a person wasn't with me, they were against me. My manager at the time didn't realize that I didn't like Remy anymore. He actually bumped into her at the Department of Motor Vehicle, and chirped me in front of her. I had no idea that he was standing in front of her when he asked me, "Guess who I'm with?"

I said "Who?"

He replied "Remy Martin". He sounded all excited over the phone. I burst his bubble and stated, "So what you telling me for? I don't like that broad". I realized that she heard me through the chirp when I heard her voice in the background. I didn't care! If she hadn't barked back, she would have looked soft in front of my manager and her entourage. We started to argue back and forth. She wanted to know why I was so mad at her. Then she sarcastically reminded me she didn't even know me. I told her she could have just said no when I asked her to be on my mixtape-simple as that. She replied that she heard I was talking shit about her at one of my shows. I told her, "Damn right, because she was a fake broad" She got mad and threatened to have Terror Squad shut my shows down.

I reminded her of her rocky relationship with Fat Joe, and how she could easily be the one Terror Squad flipped on like Fat Joe "allegedly" did Cuban Links. Then I started taunting her to go in the studio and make a song dissing me back. I didn't mind the free publicity. That conversation ended very ugly and I was seriously contemplating going to her projects in the Bronx with some goons, and stepping to her and her affiliates. I thank God I didn't follow through with that plan, because I may have been stretched out on a gurney or vice or versa. I was way too aggressive, and would have been one of those rappers that stayed in beefs. That's not what I am about. I want to unify women in the industry not perpetuate more separation. I meant well by my intentions but I was still caught up in my gangster mentality. That "get down or lay down" mindset that most urban movies portrayed was how I lived my life.

Whew! I'm so glad I changed my thinking, because look at Remy Martin. She is sitting in prison where I used to be, wondering how the hell she wound up there. My suggestion to Remy-or anyone else, who suffers from uncontrollable rage-is to seek counseling, and definitely take the Anger Management courses that the facilities offer. If I can change anyone can.

Chapter Five

Thug Love

This chapter is about all the bad choices I made with men in my life. I have the worst taste in men, which is crazy. I love Gangsters and Thugs. When I was younger, a nice, decent, hardworking guy was like a repellant to me. If it wasn't rough it wasn't right. I was head over heels for this one gangster called King Tut. He lived in the East New York section of Brooklyn, and ran shit out there. He was notorious for his gun play. Back then, you earned your street credibility by busting your gun, and getting your "body count up" (amount of murders) I was attracted to cold-blooded killers, and that was that. We understood each other. I was infatuated with guns and fast money so that is what I wanted to be around. My husband was doing his bid, and wasn't coming home any time soon; therefore, I was left alone to do me. I held him down with visits, money and packages. Plus I never missed a conjugal visit, but I still had another life in the street. He had eleven years to do and I was very young. Although I began a relationship with a female I still loved my guys.

This particular gangster Tut had recently been released from prison. All the guys I dealt with at that time were ex-convicts. I was feeling him hard, but he looked at me as a little girl. I was determined to change his mind. I would do anything to make him see I was a ride or die chick. I wanted to impress him badly.

One day, he gave me a call, telling me to meet him around his way because he wanted me to handle something for him. He had gotten word that a guy on his team was a snitch, and he wanted to get rid of him. He told me to handle it for him. I was so excited because, I was finally going to earn my brownie points. He had called the dude, and told him to meet him on Linden Boulevard. He wanted me to go into the store, buy a soda, and replace it with the .357 pistol he gave me. After that, I was supposed to walk across the street, flirt with the guy, then pull the gun out of the bag and blow his brains out. As casual as that sound was as nonchalant as the murder plan was in the process of being executed. I didn't break into a sweat, and my heart didn't skip a beat. I had no soul after my mother's death, so the idea of someone dying was almost funny to me. I figured everybody should die- young or old- because my mother did. I was mad at God, and angry at the world; therefore, I was ready to kill or be killed at any moment. I've always said I wasn't afraid of death, because I would get to be with my mother again. I still feel that way. I didn't get a chance to experience having a mother without the drama. The bitterness I felt from her death made the idea of killing that guy enjoyable. I was a messed up in the head and totally twisted.

I walked across the street with the burner in the bag. I was ready to shoot. I remember feeling numb and anxious to get it over with, so that I could go boosting later on that day. I spotted the target sitting in his vehicle and I advanced toward my prey. I got five feet away from him and I noticed Tut jogging up to the car. He gave me a signal to abort. I veered off to the right and walked away from the target. He told me later that five O (police) was cruising the boulevard, so he called off the hit. I was so sick in the head that I didn't realize my good fortune. I had the nerve to be mad at him for stopping me, because I wanted so badly to impress him. To this day, I thank God that I didn't do any harm to that poor guy. Not only would I have still been in prison, but his death would have been on my conscience. I didn't have a conscience at that time, but I developed and matured since my wild teen years. I know I would have been haunted. I also think that Tut was testing me to see if I was really "bout it" (a stand up individual). Once he saw that I was the real deal and he could count on me, he called the hit off. I thank him tremendously for reversing that situation, because that small action spared that guy's life and saved mine. As of this writing Tut is in Federal Prison serving a life sentence for a crime he didn't commit.

Also, there was an article in a hip-hop magazine, alleging that he was one of the gunmen who shot and robbed Tupac at Quad Studios. Over the years, he has maintained his innocence. But when you're notorious for certain behavior, you can easily become the fall guy for crimes you didn't commit. You can get away with one thing and, down the line, take the slack for something else. The Justice System is not a joke. You can rarely beat it.

I would do anything for attention and a thug's love. I used to love playing Bonnie and Clyde with Squirrel He was a stick-up kid and known for robbing the local drug dealers in other projects. We would drive around until he spotted a lone dealer in front of a building selling drugs. Most likely he knew that the "Vic" (victim) wouldn't have a gun on him so that was our target. My role was to distract him by flirting with him while he snuck up behind him and 'threw the drop on him with the heat" (pulled out the gun and robbed him) or stay in the car, waiting to "peel off" (drive fast) and get away. I loved those escapades it was the thrill and the excitement of living lawlessly that I craved from a thug. Years later, my husband was released from prison after doing eleven years of his sentence and I was so happy. I had broken up with Goldie a year prior to his release. She understood because I made it clear to every woman that I was ever in a relationship with that I was married and would not leave my husband for anyone. They all tried, but to no avail. My loyalty is unwavering, but to be honest, he didn't appreciate it at all. The day before his release I rented a Marriot Hotel suite and filled it with every type of designer clothes imaginable that he would need. I got him everything from Pelle Pelle, and Andrew Marc leather jackets to North Face gooses. I also got him various sneakers, shoes, and Timberland boots. I even got him a variety of colognes, and name brand wallets. Not to mention over thirty outfits. Everything a person would need in terms of personal belongings to start their life again after a decade of imprisonment. He thanked me by smacking me so hard on the second day that he was home, that my vision blurred momentarily. I was devastated! We had an argument and I guess he didn't like how I was talking to him. I had a habit of saying what's on my mind. He couldn't adjust to the new and mature me. In his eyes, I was still his little "monkey" as he affectionately called me. What a nickname, huh? That was another one of his ploys to mess with my self–esteem. I put him out of my ride and left him standing on a curb in Manhattan. I was done! Enough was enough and I wasn't going to take it anymore. I didn't answer his calls and was serious about not taking him back. I couldn't believe that after all those year, he still wanted to put his hands on me. He didn't change at all and I was heartbroken. After swearing to God that I would never go back to him, I got weak and met with him. He was so apologetic, and I decided to give him another chance. If I hadn't made up with him, my daughter would have never been conceived. For that reason I am happy I gave in. The torment was worth bringing my beautiful daughter into the world. My entire pregnancy was tumultuous. He treated me like I was a chick that he'd just met and tricked him into having his baby. I didn't feel like his loyal wife that stood by him when others had abandoned him, and I didn't feel like he was happy about the baby. He continued to hit me throughout my pregnancy. One time he choked me so hard that I frantically clawed at his face, trying to get him to loosen his grip so that my baby could get her air supply. I began to hate him with a passion and dropped into a deep depression. I cried almost every day of my pregnancy, and he would say, "I don't care about those tears, Toka. You're a f***ing cry baby" Who says that to an emotional, pregnant woman? I was hurt to my heart, because he had absolutely no compassion towards me. I craved for, but he wouldn't cater to me. He wouldn't even massage my swollen feet. If I craved a snack, I had to wobble down the steps of our duplex and get it for myself. Yet, I still woke up 4:00 a.m. every morning to fix his lunch for work. I didn't understand why he hated me so much. I finally got my answer when he admitted to me that I had embarrassed him while he was away by having relationships with women. Also, he heard that I slept with my friend, who was a male, when he first went to prison. I couldn't believe that he held on to that grudge from ten years ago, or that he didn't give me credit for not leaving him for dead. So what I was with women? I still took care of him. I even had my lover buy him sneakers and drive me to visit him. She did it due to the love she had for me; although it hurt to see me love him so much. I realized that he had too much hate stored inside of him for me, and our marriage would never work.

The day he choked me and almost caused my baby to be born mentally challenged, I'd had enough of his abuse. I chased him down our block with a butcher knife. I was intent on trying to kill him. After that incident, I had my friend call his parole officer, and tell her what was going on. I requested he be removed from our duplex in Jamaica Estates. The codes I lived by in the streets, dictated that I was violating by calling the authorities. I was simply going to have to go against the grain. I was tired and fed up. I had my friend, Paul, substitute for him in my Lamaze classes. He was like a father to me and was honored to be my Lamaze partner. I hustled my entire pregnancy, but the last two months, I was on bed rest due to having a low lined placenta. I was considered a high risk pregnancy. Goldie stayed with me, and took care of me for those last months. I don't know how I would have made it without her. He never even called to check up on me. I was overdue and went into the hospital so that the doctor could induce my labor. While I was suffering with the worst pains humanly imaginable, he came strolling into my room with headphones on and a newspaper under his arm. That hateful man sat by the window and asked me when the baby was coming, because he had some where to be. The audacity! My heart beat accelerated, and I totally lost it. I cursed him out so bad that the nurse told him he had to leave, because he was upsetting me, and the baby was in danger. I was near hysteria, and at risk of complicating my labor. After he left, the nurse was still mad about the situation. She had never seen anybody act as callous and mean. I was so embarrassed that he was my husband.

The next day, I was overcome with emotion after our baby was born, so I called him, and asked him to come to see our beautiful daughter. He came and cursed me out. I never felt so low in my life. I had just gone through fourteen hours of labor with my first and only child, and he was verbally assaulting me. What a jerk! Then he stormed out of the room. I saw the look of pity in eyes of my roommate and her boyfriend. I could have died. That day was the start of my Post-partum Depression. I never told anybody this, but I contemplated killing my beloved daughter when I was released from the hospital. I didn't know why, but I couldn't stop visualizing me drowning her while I bathed her, or throwing her down into the incinerator in my grandmother's building. I was horrified at my thoughts and trapped in my nightmares. In fear of judgment I couldn't share what I was going through with no one. I didn't even tell Queenie! She was the person who convinced me to have my baby, because I never planned to bring a child into this world while I was hustling. At the time, I didn't know that I was suffering from a disorder called Post-partum Depression, which affected a lot of mothers during post child birth. I happened to catch a segment of Oprah, where I saw the supermodel, Brooke Shields, and it was my "aha!" moment as Oprah would say. I totally identified with what she described about her spiraling depression and thoughts of suicide. She spoke of wanting to deliberately crash into a wall while driving with her baby. She also spoke about the disconnection she'd felt towards her newborn. I started crying and felt such a relief. I wasn't crazy after all. What I had been feeling was affecting a superstar too and I was so grateful she spoke about her condition. I didn't take medication for my condition, but, from that day on, my mind was strong enough to ignore the horrific urges and fight off the depression.

I know I am strong mentally, because I battled that depression by myself and didn't harm my child. It was by the grace of God, and my two angels who protect me; my mother and god mother. I went on to have a healthy relationship with my baby and, like a fool I started seeing her dad again. However, I noticed that he wasn't bonding with our daughter. She was very light-skinned when she was born, and I felt like that bothered him. His friends were dropping innuendos about her not being his child due to her complexion. So I offered to take a DNA test and, of course, I let him have it. I told him he was not a NBA star or millionaire who I was scheming to pin a child on. He had absolutely nothing and, therefore; it was senseless to put a child that wasn't his on him. I didn't care if she was a shade of green, she was his child, and I was insulted to say the least. His mother told him that she knew instantly that my daughter was a Washington (their last name) just by her hands and ears. That seemed to satisfy him. He is a big mama's boy and his mother's opinion held weight. After that discussion he didn't bother with the DNA test. He realized that his mother's great, great grandfather was a white man, and the same was with my mother. The generational genes just kicked in. I thought Velvet was adorable and loved her complexion.

I had her name picked out since I was sixteen, and I knew that I was going to marry her dad. His government name is Victor. He already had a daughter named Victoria so the next best V name was Velvet. Victor L. Washington, known to the streets as Secret Squirrel, was my childhood sweetheart, and is currently my ex-husband. He was arguably the worst mistake of my life, but the fact that he helped give my precious daughter life makes him my greatest Thug love.

The worst Thug love was a man I call Crax. He was, of course, a con who had recently been released from prison after doing a seven year bid. Not only was he a convict but a con artist, too. He ran game on me from the information I supplied him. Never tell a man how another man mistreats you, because he will know what to say and do to get into your mind and heart. In other words, he knew from me venting to him that I was abused and simply needed love, so he played Mr. Charming. That man was as slick as oil, and just as black. He reminded me of Seal the pop star, and I thought he was handsome in a tribal sort of way. Crax played me like a violin. He listened to me and treated me with such respect. He also showered me with compliments he knew I craved. He was the perfect gentleman and I loved it.

My ego and self-esteem was crushed by my husband, and I needed to be built back up. I can't blame my condition on my youth. At that point, I was an adult, and had done nine years of time in the penitentiary. I added all of my bids and came up with that sum. I was horrified! I was wiser and harder, but emotionally, I was still healing and he "got me".

I loved this guy with all my heart and soul. I would have trusted him with my life. He treated me like how I wanted my husband to treat me. It was a whirlwind romance. After six months, I was ready to marry him, but I was still legally married. At that point

I was finished with my marriage, we were separated and he kept threatening me. He found out I had cheated on him with a younger guy, who I had an affair with before I started seeing Crax. I was going through so much drama with him. I just wanted to be left alone to enjoy my new relationship. Crax and I did everything together, and I felt whole again. I was the best thing that had ever happened to him. We hustled together, and I upgraded his wardrobe. His whole swagger changed. It was all good in the beginning, but it was too good to be true.

He started staying out late, or not coming in at all. Of course, I thought he was cheating on me. I just knew he was creeping, and I was so hurt about the obvious. I mean, our sex life seemed perfect, so I couldn't understand why. When I approached him about it, he would deny it, and swear on his mama that he wasn't cheating. Well, come to find out, he was creeping around, but he wasn't sleeping with a woman. He was sucking on a glass dick! Yup, the dude was an undercover crack head. I couldn't believe it 'my bad luck! I thought to myself, how did that happen to me again? First it was with a girl, and now it was with him. Me!? Fly ass Mack Mama in love with a real live Crack head. Come to find out, this dude was robbing all the local dealers in his hood, late at night, and taking their crack and smoking it. He was a beast! He had everyone in his projects scared of him. He was known for being crazy and a smoker who everybody knew. I was the last one to find out. I had become a laughing stock. I was so in love that I didn't leave him when I found out his addiction. I tried to stick with him and help, but that's one of my biggest faults. I'm a bleeding heart and it always bites me in the butt. I made him go to a rehab. He did sixty days and came home and immediately relapsed.

I was at my wits end, so I sent him to my beautiful house in Ohio. I hustled hard to pay the bills and mortgage on my four bedroom spread in Columbus, Ohio. I stayed on the road, most of the time, to maintain my property; therefore I just used it as a vacation spot. Crax ruined it! After a week of solitude, he began to complain about how I abandoned him and left him out there by himself. I was busy in New York, trying to make money and take care of my business. I didn't have time to baby sit an addict. I was so embarrassed and hurt by the whole situation, and it got worst! He began stealing things from my house and selling it at the local 7 Eleven. I lived in a swank, upscale neighborhood in the Midwest and my Caucasian neighbors weren't used to that type of behavior. There were only two African-American families in the entire neighborhood. So he stood out like a sore thumb. I knew enough was enough when the president of the Block Association called my phone and told me about the meeting they had in reference to my houseguest. Apparently, he was menacing the neighbors by knocking on their doors, trying to borrow money. I mean, Come on! ☹

He met a white girl out there, and had the audacity to have sex with her in my bed. I think she turned him on to some mushrooms. He had to be high when he called me and tried to extort me for the deed to my house. The man I loved and thought was my Prince Charming had turned into my worst nightmare. I was going to enter my home with both guns blazing, but, thankfully, Queenie took care of it for me. Over the years, she had changed her life and became a law abiding citizen. She handled that maniac like citizens do. She called the police, and they came to apprehended him. This fool actually had a stand-off with the police. He didn't want to open the door to my house and give himself up. Ohio showed him a thing or two about how serious they take their law enforcement. They brought the "bird" (helicopter) out, and a truck filled with a S.W.A.T. team. The tactical unit knocked down my front door and dragged him out of my house. He was unarmed and lucky, because they would have roughed him up good for being ignorant.

When he arrived back in New York, he was detained in our prison system. That's when he got the nerve to write a letter to Squirrel. My ex-husband is very well-known in the system, which is the result of the many years he spent in prison. It wasn't hard to contact him. Crax told him that I was trying to get him to "merk" (kill) him for me. He also said that I was a lousy mother, and a bunch of other crappy lies. Of course, Squirrel went for that foolishness and, to this day, he doesn't trust me with his address. He swears that I was trying to "off-him." I told him not to listen to the ramblings of a disgruntled addict.

As much pain as I have endured from my daughter's father, I would never want to hurt him, and most of all, hurt my daughter. She loves her father. Lord knows, if I would have plotted his assassination, I would be sitting in prison right now, serving a life sentence. Crax would have certainly turned me in for conspiracy to murder. I was so furious at him for spreading those nasty lies. I had my goons, who were in the same prison take care of him for me. He wears that scar- of- shame to this day. I lived by the code: Death before dishonor! I am so glad that I denounced that lifestyle and found my conscience, because I would most likely be dead right now.

It is a dark, ugly world, and I possess a light that shines in me. I don't want my legacy to be what I was known for in the streets. That's why I've made the decision to change my life; however I can't change the past or my mistakes. I want to be forgiven as I forgive and, by baring my soul in this tell all, I am cleansing my spirit. I have to stay away from people, places and things that trigger my addictions. Thugs no longer appeal to me. I am looking for a nice, clean-cut professional guy, to marry, and enjoy the rest of my life with. I may shop for a reality show called "Mack looking for Love not Thugs". I want an intelligent, classy man, with no ties to the underworld. I would prefer an athlete, because I love a sexy, muscular body. Until then I will concentrate on my career, and enjoy life. God will do the picking for me and send me an angel.

Chapter Six

MACK MAMA

I can't remember who named me Mack Mama, but I do remember why. I had a white girl named Krissy working for me. She was a runaway from West Virginia. My friend Pam brought her up to New York when she returned from a family vacation. Krissy was only fifteen years old. I was eighteen years old, getting plenty of money, and still wilding out in the streets. She couldn't stay with Pam, so I took her in, and taught her how to steal. On the strength of her skin color, it was like having a stealing pass. I would go in the stores, load up four bags, and hide them under the racks. Then I would tell her where they were located and she would scoop up the goods and waltz right out the door. In fact, the security guards would hold the door open for her, and bid her a nice day. I thought it was hilarious. It goes to show you how race plays a big part in every aspect of society, especially crime.

After boosting, she would be bored, and wanted to have sex. I let the guys, who were lusting over my "white girl", pay me to have sex with her. I didn't even realize that I was macking or pimping her out. I didn't want her to have sex for free. She was so dizzy that she didn't care. She was good as long as she got off. I didn't even bother to give her money, because I housed her, fed her and kept her in nice clothes. She had never been treated so good. She was poor, white trash, and ran away from an abusive father who molested her. I felt sorry for the poor thing until she tried to play me. She used to call me Mama she would say "Mama I love yooo" in her country accent. I grew fond of old Krissy until she started falling in love with one of her tricks. She decided to leave me and move in with him. I lost it! I beat her with a belt like she was my child. I whooped her good, until she turned beat red.

That is something that I regret to this day. I was no better than her father, who abused her for years. That girl loved and worshipped me for treating her so well but, as soon as she betrayed me I resorted to violence. I was furious at her for sneaking behind my back with the dude, and he was planning on taking her from me, and pimping her on the street. I tried to explain that to her, but she didn't believe me. The next day, I woke up, and Krissy was gone. She stole a thousand dollars and my rental car. She left me a note that read something like this:

"Mama, I love you, but I can't take no more 'beatins'. I left my paw cuz' he beat on me, and I hated it. I'm sorry for taking the money and the car, but I needed it to get on the road. I believed you when you said that these boys just want to sell me, but so do you. Thank you for all you done, but I gotta' go now. I will never forget you pleez' don't be mad with me. I just couldn't take it anymore. I will pay you back one day.

Love always, Krissy"

That letter messed me up. I couldn't even be mad at her about the money or the car. I had lost my Krissy. I made so much money off of her, and actually cared for her. I didn't want anyone to abuse her, but inadvertently, I became the bad guy. Mack Mama was born. After that, I tried not to mistreat any of my girls. I was taught a valuable lesson that cost me a lot of money. When I was a teenager, I was lost in the source. I had too much bitterness and rage bottled up inside of me. It made me react to certain situations in an extreme manner.

The first girl I went out with, who I called my girlfriend was a hustler I called AJ. Her game was picking pockets for money. She would go on the trains at rush hour and get the business men for their wallets and envelopes filled with cash. She did so well that I stopped boosting and she took care of me. We moved into a very upscale duplex, located in downtown Brooklyn.

We were only seventeen years old and living quite lovely. The rent was fifteen- hundred dollars, and back then, that was high, but we did it. I loved that crib. We had three bathrooms; two of them had marble from the wall to the floor, with brass and crystal fixtures. The lower level was big enough to be another apartment, with a patio garden, washing machine and dryer. The thing was, we were living way above our means. We relied on hustling to pay our bills, and she was having a bad streak. She told me she was going to receive a large inheritance from her father, so I wasn't worried about the rent, until I found out that she was lying. It was all a fantasy that she'd made up. She just wanted to impress me. She didn't even have a default plan. When I noticed the money was taking too long to come, I asked her mother about it, and the "spot was blown up" (revealed) she had no idea what I was talking about. I was livid! After six months of struggling to pay our bills we finally had to leave and move in with Queenie.

I hated AJ's guts after that. I contemplated throwing her out of the window, but settled on beating her with an extension cord and dousing her welts with alcohol. I tortured her because she lied to me about that money and we lost my dream crib. I needed to be stopped, because I had lost my mind. You know what's crazy? When I did my first extensive bid upstate, which was four-and- a-half years, she stuck by my side, and took care of me. She was a very loyal to me and I regret how I treated that girl. One time, I pulled a gun out on her when she tried to stop me from going out on a date with her friend. I was head over heels for her friend. I started dating her eventually leaving AJ. When I went to prison on my first extensive bid the girl left me and told me she couldn't do all that time with me. She broke my heart and, to add insult to injury, she had another woman in my bed. Amazingly, AJ took me back knowing that I had all of that time. She was still in love with me and I was very grateful. I apologized to her, wooing her back on a visit, while I was in Bedford Hills Correctional Facility. She accepted my apology and took care of me my entire bid. I didn't want or need anything. That's why I think it took so long for me to quit the illegal side of hustling. At that point I had not learned my lesson nor hit rock bottom. All throughout my bids, I was very well cared for, and had any luxury that was afforded in jail. It's important to feel hard time, but I never really felt it.

I was popular in every prison. I had all the "creature comforts"(the little things that make you comfortable in jail) like a lot of clothes, footwear, music, a television, a locker full of commissary, and , of course, money on my books. That's all you need to live comfortably in prison. I would like to advise parents that have out- of- control kids, who are in prison, not to send anything but cosmetics: no money, no sneakers or anything extra. That will make the bid unbearable. They will think long and hard before they do anything that will get them in trouble and sent back. I swear I wish my first bid would have been hard, because I might not have gotten caught up in recidivism. (The cycle of repeat incarceration that the prison systems rely on to continue making money). The only part of going through the system that left a lasting impression on me is the feel of handcuffs on my wrist, and the jarring sounds of the cells clanking shut. I feel very claustrophobic in small spaces. I get instant flash backs of being shackled and locked up. There is no greater degradation than a human being who is bound with steel handcuffs and leg shackles. I wouldn't wish prison on my worst enemy. Not to mention being bossed around by people who are in some cases no better than you are. I have a problem being told what to do and when to do it, because of my prison experiences.

I was involved in an altercation with this girl named Rose Hunt, who was known for cutting people. She was treacherous, but she'd finally met her match. I had cut her in self-defense in front of a popular club called the "Q Club". After the party, she tried to attack me with a butcher knife, but I managed to slash her back when she drunkenly fell to the ground. Two drunks fighting is a lethal combination. She was supposed to be gangster chick, but squealed like a pig. She had me and Queenie locked up. Queenie was with me outside the club. She had kicked Rose in her butt when she tried to attack us with the butcher knife. We were drunk and thought she was a joke. Rose had messed up when she started talking junk to Queenie about another one of our associates, that she happened to be beefing with. The incident could have been avoided, but you don't approach O.B.G's with some bullshit and expect to walk away without getting stomped out. It wasn't happening back in 'dem days. Not a chance! I have the patience to negotiate and sign peace treaties now but back then I had zero tolerance.

After being on the run for a year, I was apprehended for the assault. Rose had lied on me, throwing in a robbery charge, claiming that I took a silver broach from her. What hood rat wore broaches? I tried to explain that to the detectives, but they weren't trying to hear me. The charges got stuck and I was sent up north with a sentence of 1 ½ to 4 ½ years. I did 2 ½, came back home, and went back on two parole violations back to back. The first violation was for 7 months, and the second one was for 8 months. Altogether I did 45 months on that bid. The parole board thought I was a threat to society, and Rose didn't want me released. When she was notified by Parole of my upcoming release, she told them that she feared for her life. I tried to tell the Parole Board that It was done in self-defense, but it fell on deaf ears. I was hit with 12 months. It was a blessing in disguise, because I discovered my talent for music in prison. I wouldn't be where I am today if it wasn't for that bid. I am finally over the fact that she snitched on me, which I'd rather she had retaliated. I was so brainwashed with the street code that I wanted her to try and cut me back rather than send me to jail. That sounds so ridiculous now. I hated that girl for a long time. When I came home, and bumped into her, we had a big argument. I knew she was going to have me locked up again, so I had a trick for her. I beat her to the punch and had one of my friends have her arrested for a trumped up charge. I wanted her to feel what I felt when I went to Jail. She bailed out of Rikers Island and told everybody that I snitched on her. 'Aint that a b***h! I had done 4 ½ years behind her ratting on me, but I was the snitch!? She chose the weapon for the battle when she took it to the police. I showed her how it felt, yet I was the bad guy?

I'm so happy that part of my life is over. It was all so retarded when I look back on my life. I wasted valuable years with that street mentality and dealing with undesirables who made me as lowly as they were. If only I could rewind the hands of time. I would bring my mother back, healthy and sober/I would wake up and the nightmare is over… (Verse from "Miss You Mama")

I bumped into Grimy on Rikers Island. I had to deal with the beef that we had from when I had shot her. She had the whole jail against me. It was crazy! She was feeding all the dope fiends and crack heads drugs that she smuggled in on her visits. That made her the "Man" (the one who called the shots). I was already distraught over having to go upstate and do so much time; therefore, I didn't want to be bothered with the Grimey situation. I tried to avoid the drama.

It didn't work. I was forced to bring the beast out. I was walking from the chow hall one day, and a group of chicks stopped me. One crazy-looking girl named Jamaica approached me. She told me that I couldn't pass an imaginary line that she had drawn, because someone told her that I had stolen her sneakers. Now, I knew that was a joke. I had about four pair of crisp kicks under my bunk, so I knew that she was trying to punk me. Then she claimed to be Grimey's cousin, which made it all click. Grimy had put a hit out on me for shooting her. At that point, I knew that in order for the bullshit to stop, I had to fight her, and whoever else Grimey sent after me. So, I stopped talking and trying to explain that I had no need to steal her sneakers and abruptly punched her in the face. A good old fashioned sucker punch, that she didn't see coming. All hell broke loose. We were thumping in that long hallway. All I wanted to do was get back to Dorm 20, and lay on my bunk in peace, but I was fighting for my respect. My friend Rush who was a hermaphrodite jumped into the fight. She fractured the girl's arm. She had crazy love for me. Rush looked just like a man, and was born with both sexes. She actually had a little penis. I was fascinated by that. She had a deep voice, a beard and she was a Jewish Russian girl. After that fight nobody messed with us, she was my unofficial body guard. Everybody thought she was my girl, but we weren't intimate. We always took showers together in separate stalls. One day, she showed me her genitals, but it was too weird for me. She was loyal and down for whatever. She was actually the coolest guy/ girl I had ever met. I often wonder what became of Rush.

Jamaica went out with a girl named Danny, who was a big butch. She was around 200 pounds, and had the whole jail scared of her. Even the C.O's let her get away with murder. When she heard that we jumped her girl, she sent word for us to meet her in the yard. I put about ten batteries in my sock and knotted it up. Plus I carried a pen in my pocket, ready to pluck her eyeball out of its socket. Armed to the teeth, and rolling with Big Rush, I went to the yard, ready for war. We immediately spotted Danny, Grimey and Jamaica. Everybody was outside, waiting to see the highly anticipated show down. We were the talk of the jail. I was not playing! I tried to chill, but Grimey was looking for drama. So she and her so-called fake family were going to get it. I was really pissed off that she had everybody in our business. Those girls had no idea that she had me set up and robbed. She told them one side of the story, which made me look like the villain who just up and shot poor little Grimey. I was sick of trying to explain my side of the story. I was ready to see blood. End of story! Once Grimey looked into my eyes, she wanted to squash the beef. She knew that it was going too far. Her groupies followed suit and left it alone. It was Rush and I against the entire yard, but we held our ground, and they backed off.

After that, I had no more problems. I started getting balloons filled with drugs on the visit. I sold them and became very popular. Drugs are like money in the penitentiary and, whoever has it has the power. Prison is an underground society, and it never fails to amaze me. Women who have never been gay in their lives come to jail and have relationships with girls, and get so possessive and territorial about their "bulldaggers" or AG's It's rare to see two feminine women together in jail. Most of the time, the girl is looking for a replacement for a man. It's very rare to find genuine lesbians; basically, the bulldaggers are the boy types, and more dominant in the relationship. So, you have a society of women who are walking around, holding hands, and very much "In love". They also go into jealous rages, because their partners began to act like "pacman" (Making out with multiple girls) which causes major beefs between the lovers. It's a madhouse in prison. There is nothing but negativity and drama in that world. I hated every moment. It felt like hell on earth.

I was on Riker's Island when it was a big playground. I would loiter in the halls, sell my product, and walk around like I was on the block. Unbelievable! At nineteen years old, I learned absolutely nothing positive by being in jail. I was only taught how to excel in corruption. It was not until I was transferred upstate that I got something out of doing that bid. I found my musical talent when I went upstate to Albion Correctional Facility and got into a fight with these girls in my dorm. I was placed in the SHU (Segregated Housing Unit), where you were sent when you got into trouble. I loved the confinement. I was able to think and create. That's where I realized I had a knack for rapping. I loved Biggie, plus he was from Brooklyn. I saw my homeboys, in Biggie's "Juicy" video and lost my mind. The same hood cats who I used to chill with on the streets were on television, and they got there because of rapping. Shit, you couldn't tell me nothing, I was determined to write a rap song and blow up. I was so idealistic back in those days. If I had realized how difficult it was to get into the music industry, I would have started painting or drawing portraits instead. Real talk!

I went to college in that prison, and was on the Dean's list. I maintained a 4.0 grade point average. I loved it! That's when I realized that I was a great public speaker. I excelled in that course, and knew that speaking before an audience was a breeze for me. It was very difficult for the other women in my class, but, it was simple for me. I loved to get attention; therefore, it was easy for me to perform in front of groups of people. As much as I hated being locked up, I considered that bid as being my training camp. I received all of my education in the prison system. When I was sixteen, I obtained my G.E.D. on my first bid. I was very intelligent, so educating myself behind the walls was a given. I used to study the dictionary for the purpose of expanding my vocabulary when I speak. When you have nothing but time on your hands, you can use it productively or foolishly; it's however you choose to do your time.

When I was released from prison my rap moniker was Miss CoCo, because a few of my friends called me CoCo. However, people got me confused with Dj CoCo Chanel from Hot 97, so I changed it. I decided to use Mack Mama because that's who I was. I macked the hustling game and lived lovely off of it. Plus, I had just copped a brand new Beamer (BMW), and was feeling real Mackalicious. I went with that handle and it stuck. I swore up and down that when I came home, I would concentrate on my music career. I had found something that I was good at doing, and it was legal. I figured it would be a breeze, because I knew Understanding who was known as Undeas in the music business. He was Biggie's business partner at the time and my ex-lover. During my entire bid, I banked on him putting me on. It was a no-brainer. When we were together, I used to look out for him, boosting him fly gear, which was no easy feat, considering his size. He was at least two-hundred-and-fifty pounds. One outfit and my girdle would be full. He had blew up in the Industry and, with Biggie being a superstar rapper I just knew it was a place on the team for me. Lil Kim was the hottest female emcee in the game, while doing her thing with Undeas Recording. So, why wouldn't the Original Bad Girl get a shot? Well, I had a rude awakening. I had my homegirl, Tracy, take me to the Hit Factory, where Un was recording Charlie Baltimore's album. She had just signed to his label. I waltz up in there in my full-length, skin on skin, swing mink, and diamonds "blinging" like I belonged in that b***h. Everybody in the studio was wondering who I was until I spotted a familiar face. It was Un's brother Justice. "Hey Jus! what's up, boo?"

"Oh shit! What's going on, Matoka?" We exchanged greetings and broke the ice. I peeped Charlie Baltimore checking me out, but I didn't skip a beat. I wanted to see Un, and I was on a mission. "Where's Un at? I asked. There was a slight pause, and everyone just looked at me funny. So, me being me, I repeated myself a little louder. **WHERE 'DAT 'NICCA AT!? TELL HIM I'M OUT HERE!"** I had no idea that it was a protocol that I had to go through to see the big boss, because he was still "Understanding from Fulton and Washington, who worked for Uncle Bennie at the Coke spot" to me. "He's sleeping Ma," Justice responded. "Oh, well, wake that 'nicca up! Shit, I just came home. I need to see him," I demanded. I knew he wouldn't have a problem waking up for "me". I hadn't seen him for about six years, but I didn't change, and I didn't think he did either. Justice took me into the other room and, there he was, looking colossal. It seemed like he took up the entire room, while laid out sleeping. He was a big dude, and very intimidating, but not to me. I walked right over and tapped him on the shoulder. "Eh, boo, wake up. Wake up. UN! It's me, MATOKAAA," I sung excitedly, because I had been dreaming about that moment. I knew it was fittin' to be on and poppin'. He seemed to grumble like a huge bear. Then he cracked one eye open with a grimace on his face. He stared at me for a moment. It seemed like time had stopped, and everybody was waiting to see what his reaction was going to be; since apparently no one dared to wake his majesty up. "Oh! What up, Matoka?" he greeted. With that simple greeting, the air seemed to clear, and the tension disappeared.

I knew that it was going to be straight once he realized who I was. He gave me a slow smile that looked more like apprehension than happiness to see me. As I think about it now, he probably was thinking, 'What the hell this wild bitch want?' he knew how crazy I was, and didn't want no parts of that foolishness around him. He was a big time record executive, and I was still a hood rat from Brooklyn in his eyes.

"I rap now, boo! I go by the name Mack Mama. I want you to hear my music" I gushed excitedly. Back then, I was so naive when it came to the music industry. I didn't know that you had to be a certain way when you're dealing with the business. I only knew one way to be, and that was "real". So, I didn't bother to act nonchalant or humble. I said what was on my mind. I wanted In! He took me into the studio, played my music, and everybody listened silently. There was no head-bopping or enthusiasm whatsoever. I was slowly feeling my dream slip away. He didn't like my music.

I was crushed but I didn't show it. He told me that he had Charlie Baltimore, and wasn't looking for another female artist, but he'll pass my demo along to other Labels. I looked at him in disbelief. He was actually dismissing me! I wanted to bust him in his big head, but I smiled, told him that I understood, and bowed out gracefully. My pride wouldn't let him see my tears. I swear that when I was leaving, I saw Charlie Baltimore smirk at me. At that moment, I hated her, and wanted to beat her ass. I needed to take my disappointment and sadness out on someone, but I wouldn't have given them the satisfaction of saying "See, that's why I'm not dealing with that street b***h" It always gave me a slight satisfaction that Charlie Baltimore's album never came out. I would say, "See, that 'nicca Un should have signed me," but everything happens for a reason. First of all, I wasn't as nice lyrically as I am now, so, in all fairness, he wasn't impressed with the music. I felt that on the strength of the connection we had, and the fact that I had been recently released from prison, trying to do something positive, he should have gave me a job.

Secondly, I would have been involved with the drama that surrounded Un and his rise and fall in the industry. His whole camp fell off. His situation really went downhill after he allegedly leaked Jay-Z's album. Then he sued Jay-Z for allegedly stabbing him. You better believe that Undeas and, whoever was associated with him, was blackballed in the industry. I was a little discouraged but still determined to make it. I wanted to show Un and all the non-believers, that I was going to become a star. The only problem was my addiction to money. I didn't want to be a starving artist. I wanted to hustle, and drive the fancy cars, and wear the diamonds and furs that the stars wore. That's what I was used to, and I didn't want to give up my lifestyle to concentrate on music. I felt that I lived like a star, so I deserved to be one. Society felt like I was a crook, and I deserved to be behind bars. I wouldn't succeed until I realized that. By then, I stopped boosting and stepped my game up to credit card fraud. I loved it! It was my new addiction. It was so easy. No more sneaking around the store and stealing. Without the hassle of a bulging girdle or suspicious security guard, I shopped and walked out of any store with my bags. I really thought that I was spending "my" money, and would become indignant if the cashier gave me any grief. I had the credit card holder's personal information and matching identification. I had convinced myself that I was that person. What a sickness. I lived in this fantasy world for years destroying credit, and living the lifestyle of a rich person. There was nothing I wanted that I couldn't get. That is why when the law finally caught up to me, they gave me plenty of time, to think about my actions. I learned the meaning of remorse in prison. Especially as I write my memoir. I am reliving the insanity that I called my life and it seems so unreal to me. As if I am sitting here creating a fictional story. I am in shock and filled with remorse and regret. That is how I know I have changed.

I had gotten arrested too many times in my BMW. It was leased and, by then, the corporate office had enough of my irresponsible behavior. I was living wild and reckless and didn't care. Six months later, I bought a brand new ML320 Benz truck. You couldn't tell me anything. All I did was recruit workers. I loved Caucasian men because they got away with murder. Society thinks if its white it's right, and that philosophy causes corporate America to get swindled most of the time. Some white folks are the biggest crooks. My favorite employee and partner in crime was a middle-aged Jewish guy named Paul. He looked like Willie Nelson- the country crooner- when I first met him. He had a long, salt-and-pepper pony tail and a beard that hung down to his chest. By the time I transformed his appearance, he could have passed for a judge or a doctor. I gave him a five-star makeover that was complete with a haircut and brand new, fancy wardrobe. I had him looking and feeling like new money. Then we would tear the malls up. He couldn't believe how easy it was for him use credit cards without producing additional identification, and then leave the stores with thousands of dollars in merchandise. I, on the other hand, would get the fish-eye treatment on occasions just because I was black. He was boggled by it because he didn't have a prejudice bone in his body, and had hung out with black and latino people for years. I loved him for that. I used to say he was black in a white man's body.

For years, we were like zombies. We did nothing but hustle from the time the stores opened to the moment they closed. We lived on the road. We got arrested one time for our greed. My car was so loaded with shopping bags and merchandise that we couldn't see out of the back window. That should have made us leave the mall, but it didn't, so we ended up getting busted. I had my people bail Paul out first; that way, he could go hustling to get the money to bail me out. That's how close we were, and how loyal we were to each other. That was my partner in crime, and I love him. He has passed away and it breaks my heart. He succumbed to cancer Nov 13th 2011. In the first edition of this memoir I wrote *"He has lung cancer*

now…I'm praying that he beat it and lives to see my career take off. He invested so much into my dreams and I want to be able to take care of him. He is 66 years old and the strongest man I know".
Unfortunately, he did not make it. He was able to read the first edition of my book and he was very proud of me. I am so relieved that he died knowing that I am still following my dreams, and I am making them come true. We spent years on the road discussing how I wanted to break into the music industry. He would forgo his cut of the money we made, on many occasions, just so I could use it for studio time or pay my exuberant bills. I love Paul Harnik. He will be missed. ☹

I had put my music on hold, using the excuses that I wanted to do it big like Master P and Brian "Birdman" Williams, from Cash Money. I kept telling myself I needed to grind to get more money so that I could be the first female to come out independently with my own label: O.B.G. Records. I was inspired by all the drug dealers that were in the music business, financing there companies by hustling. That was my goal and I was on a mission. Everybody knew that I was Mack Mama because I would go in the studio and churn out mix tapes on my off time. I loved making music just as much as I loved making money. I was extremely cocky and felt that all the female rappers that were in the rap game, and came from Brooklyn, were rapping about me. My real life experiences, was the blueprint for their rhymes. That's why I started reppin' O.B.G. I made that name up in prison when I heard Lil Kim refer to herself as bad girl. Of course she was affiliated with Puffy's Label, Bad Boy Records so it was natural for her to reference herself as a Bad Girl. However, I was really in the streets busting my gun and being bad so I threw the "original" in front of it and took it from there.

When I was nine months pregnant with my daughter, I lived in a swank condo in Jamaica Estates, which was located in Jamaica, New York. You couldn't tell me anything. At that time, a few celebrities lived in that neighborhood, so it felt like I truly accomplished something worthwhile. I had a nice crib, beautiful furniture, and a luxury vehicle. Plus I had all the designer gear a girl could want, but there was one thing missing-I wanted a career. When you bring a child into the world, you start thinking about the future, and how you can provide for their life. I knew that I couldn't live off of the land forever. I didn't receive any type of public assistance. I relied solely on hustling. It was unbelievable because my sister has her Master degree, along with a career as a social worker, but she was still struggling with her bills. I felt that I had it so good, because I didn't finish college and had acquired more material possessions than she had. I conveniently forgot the occupational hazards of what I was doing. Going to prison wasn't worth the lifestyle I lived at all.

My passion for my music was not fulfilled. I needed to go hard in order to make it, and I needed someone who had connections to put me on. It's not how much talent you have it's who you know in the game. My friend Tracy was Lil Kim's assistant, and she always wanted me to hang out with them on different occasions, because she knew I wanted to get into the game. I never had the time to chill with them. I was always so busy hustling to pay my bills. I was living way beyond my means and needed to sell something to pay my rent. I went through a drought. I was getting work (credit cards) that didn't have any money on them, so I had to sell one of my mink coats to keep me afloat. I had around twenty personal furs in my collection, so I decided that I had to start liquidating.

I called Tracy and requested that she ask Kim if she was interested in buying one of my coats. Lil' Kim was interested in purchasing one, so Tracy brought me to her mini mansion in New Jersey. At that, she was still down with Junior Mafia, and a few members lived with her. It was a nice, gated community on "Rapper's Row". That was the nickname for the area she resided in, because of all the rappers that lived in that section of New Jersey, which was right over the George Washington Bridge.

Kim had a fabulous place. I did a quick scan as I entered the door and eyed the Italian marbled walls and white piano that was elegantly sitting on a raised platform in her living room. Then I noticed the Gucci designer sofa, and the cardboard, life-size cutout of her, which was classic Lil Kim. Her dining room table sat twelve and looked like a prop from the set of The God Father. She was serious about that Junior Mafia stuff. I loved it.

We went up stairs to the third floor where her master bedroom was located, and I showed her the mink. It was a beautiful white-sheared swing, skin-on-skin, three-quarter length mink. Of course, she loved it, and wanted to buy it. Everything was going smooth until I told her that I wanted twenty-five hundred dollars for the Fur. She wanted to give me two-thousand dollars, but I wasn't budging. I felt like she was already getting a good deal. I was selling it for a third of the retail price because I had worn it a few times and, besides that, I really needed the bread. She was a celebrity figure. Twenty-five- hundred dollars should have been nothing for a star, right?

Tracy had to pull me to the side and plead with me to give her the deal. She pointed out that if I looked out for kim, she would probably help me with my rap career. That piqued my interest. I thought about it and decided that five hundred short wasn't going to kill me, but I still wanted my balance owed to me at another time. We agreed that she would give me the two grand and I would wait on the five. The business was concluded, and then we started to discuss my music. She was interested in hearing me, so I gave her a few bars:

Chicks talk about hustling, I did that shit/ Talk about being fly, I am that B***h/Talk about pushing whips, I had my shit/Before I had a flow/Before I did a show /Copped my Beamer and my Benz just to let ya' know/Original Bad Girl Like I Said Befo'...

When I got to that last part I knew I had messed up with that "Original Bad Girl" line. Kim's face told it all. It said: "Bitch you won't take my crown". Her lips gave me a phony smile. "Awww, that was good hon," she said with the smallest hint of sarcasm "Keep up the good work. You're gonna' make it". She actually said that, in her phony white girl voice. I was nine month pregnant aggravated, and two seconds away from taking my coat and the money from her little ass. That's when Tracy gave me a pleading look. I didn't want to mess things up for Tracy, because she had to work for Lil' Kim, so I gave her a pass. I should have known that she wasn't going to help another female emcee. She was a hater and wanted all the shine for herself. She looked at me and seen the threat. Even at nine months pregnant I was fly. I had on a butter-soft suede shirt, along with a pair of hot, burgundy leather pants I had got from 'A Pea in the Pod' my favorite maternity store for divas. My full-length, light brown, two-toned hooded mink was the icing on the cake. Also, she saw my Benz truck parked in her driveway and knew that I was the real deal. She was not messing with me. It's funny because God don't like ugly. She was a pretty girl even without the benefit of makeup and, earlier in the conversation she mentioned that she wanted to get her nose done. Tracy and I tried to talk her out of it, but she was hell-bent on having plastic surgery done on her face. Now, she looks nuts, and her career is over. Had she put me on her team, I would have convinced her not to do all that foolishness to her face. The body work was okay. But when God gives you natural beauty and you mess with his gift, you will be cursed and the results are irreversible. Poor thing!

That encounter with Lil Kim made me less of a fan. Then a year later, she really pissed me off. I made a mixtape called "The Realest Bitch: Volume 1". On that cd I was interviewed by my friend. Her character was Cindy Simmons. We were spoofing my favorite radio personality at that time, Wendy Williams. In the interview, I explained that I was representing for the average chicks from the hood that couldn't afford Chanel and other high-end designer labels so I said recited a piece from a verse I had:

"I can rock an Old Navy tee and still be me.

When you know who you are, You're always a star!"

That simple statement caused a lot of drama. I was selling my cd's all over the hood and happened to run into a dude name World that Kim was messing with at the time. He is well known in Brooklyn and currently locked up for numerous murders. I hit him with my cd, and I know that he let Kim hear it. What happened next caused me to lose it.

Christmas came around and I received a phone call from my ex-girlfriend, Andrell. She was all worked up over something "YO, DID YOU SEE LIL KIM'S OLD NAVY COMMERCIAL?" She yelled excitedly.

"Huh? What are you talking about? Why would Lil Kim be in an Old Navy Commercial?" I asked, and then it struck me like lightening.

"She was saying the exact same thing you said on your cd she stole your line" Andrell muttered annoyed at the audacity of Lil Kim. I was so heated. I knew that she had heard my interview. She took the concept of wearing Old Navy and still being a star to the company and they jumped on it. It was a great idea that I wanted to present to Old Navy when I came out with my album, but, yet again, my dream was shattered. I was in a rage and vowed that I would destroy the Lil' Thief. After that, I was intent on dissing her in every song I wrote. My second mixtape 'The Realest Bitch: Volume 2" was dedicated to going in on her, on damn near every track. I was obsessed

115

with killing her street cred'-at least in Brooklyn. This was before the internet was popular, so I had to literally circulate my cd's in the streets from out of my trunk. I wanted to make sure that she heard me. She never responded by saying my name, but she would say subliminal disses in a few of her verses on her underground mixtapes. She was smart. She knew if she mentioned my name-Mack Mama-I would have blown up instantly. I have since let that anger go and chalked it up as how the game goes.

That experience taught me to copyright any and all of my music, slogans, and lyrics. In business, you can't be emotional and want to fight when someone does grimey shit to you. It's a matter of making the perpetrator pay. Although I am over it, I couldn't resist one last dig on my song, "Mack Mama" where I say: "Lil' Mama, fix your makeup…" I was talking about Lil' Kim when she does the crazy thick, drawn-on eyebrows. The Lil' Mama is in reference to her being a little, miniature, wannabe me. I had to clarify that because people think I am talking about the young rapper, Lil' Mama, who I happen to like and respect. I watched her grind and come up on the underground scene; not to mention, her mentor, Paula Perry, did a song with me on my O.B.G.'s The Movement cd.

I am not a hater. I love female emcees. I am one of the only female emcee-that I know about-who released a collaborative mixtape with over twenty female emcees that spit acid. I wasn't scared to share the limelight. When you know who you are, and you're confident in your ability to be the best, you are not intimidated by others who are great. I am Mack Mama!

Me on a Visit. I was In Albion Correctional Facility 1993
You couldn't tell me nothing...lol
I Love Minks (Thanks Angie For Letting Me Rock It For The Flick...lol)

MackMama and
The Sexy Mackets
(2004)

▲ Queenie and Natoka
Throwback
16 Years Old
My Partner In Crime
Fly Girls Minked-Out...Those Were
The Good Ole Days....Chea!

▼ Natoka and Queenie 2010
Still Fly!

▲ Bliss Boogie aka Malorie Knox and Me
O.B.G.'s
Mack n' Malorie
Album Coming Soon....

◄ Lil Kisha (R.I.P) ,
Me and Tracy
(1996)

◀ Velvet's
Christening
(2002)

Me ▶
5 Months Pregs

Princess Velvet ▶
3 Yearls Old

Velvet
◀ 3rd Halloween

My Dad and Velvet ▶
8 Years Old

▲ Goldie and Me
1996

◄

Greg, Me and
T-Roy
My Childhood Friends
1998

◀ I had Swag before the term
was popular...
Pregs and all!

▶

This is when
Ellen Tracy Suits
were poppin' and
Mushroom Hairstyles
(1996)

WE MADE A GOOD
LOOKING FAMILY
(2001)

MY EX-HUSBAND
AND I...
CHILDHOOD
SWEETHEARTS

My Dearest
Friend Poochie
My #1 Fan
At One Of
My Shows
(2004)

Me and
My Baby Girl ▶

2003

◀ Nana and My Lil Sister
(Graduation)

◄ Free Mighty!
My Homie For Life
Long Live The King!
(2009)

Me and My Trainer ►
He's Responsible
For Keeping Up My
Mackalicious Body
Salute The Homie Rhythm
"Get Off My Booty Nicca...lol"
(2010)

Sparkles
and
Me Clowning
Around
(2010)

Me
"Mackin Up"
on My B-Day
in the
Halfway House
Just Outta The Clink
And Ready To Partaaay!!
(2008)

Me Being Macky
2010

◄ U Watching Me
and
I'm Watching U ... Hey Darlin
Thanks For Supporting Me
I Appreciate All The Love
And I Know You Are
Enjoying Me Right Now...Muah!!!

Chapter Seven

OHIO

I lived in Columbus Ohio for a few years. I had a beautiful home in Westerville. I wanted to raise my daughter away from the urban jungle I grew up in. I wanted her to go to school with Caucasians, and speak proper English, take ballet, piano and karate lessons. Everything, little girls should have the opportunity to do. So I packed up and moved to Ohio. Queenie lived there and encouraged me to make the move. She had retired from the streets and was heavy into real estate and commercial property. She helped me purchase a beautiful four bedroom, two-and- a- half bathroom, full basement spread. That was my biggest accomplishment and I was ecstatic. The only problem was I never got a chance to fully enjoy my home because I stayed on the road hustling hard to pay my hefty bills. I had put so much money into decorating my new home that it was ridiculous. I had professionals come in and wall paper each room with a different theme. I picked out beautiful pieces of furniture for each room. I have a knack for interior decorating, so I had a ball. My house was my sanctuary and I loved my neighborhood. It was so far removed from the concrete jungle of the projects. I jogged around my neighborhood, inhaling freedom, and it smelled great. Imagine how I felt living in the Midwest. It was a far cry from Brooklyn. My neighbors were so prejudice that in the five years I lived in my home, no one ever spoke to me. I didn't mind one bit. I wanted to be left alone; therefore, I didn't mind the antisocial neighbors. I respected the fact that they weren't smiling in my face, knowing they didn't like me because of the color of my skin.

I made my home very comfortable and had everything I needed to entertain my family. I wish I had the resources back then to simply give up my criminal lifestyle and live normal. I had lost my home and my vehicles when I went to prison on my final bid. I have nothing to show for all the years I've dedicated to the hustle. I regret all I have done in my life except for having my child, but I realize I can't erase my past. I can only move on and change my "stinking thinking"- that is a recovery term that I learned from attending Narcotics Anonymous groups in prison. As I write this memoir, I am in shock, because my mentality was seriously warped. I didn't realize that it was so crazy. It is unrealistic to think that you can live lawlessly and get away with it. After a while, you will get nabbed. I know because it happened to me.

On New Year's Eve, 2003, the worst thing that could have happened to me occurred on that day. I was arrested for robbery and kidnapping in the second degree. Now, those charges may sound like I am a lunatic, but I assure you that I am not. I warn anybody who even considers doing a crime in Ohio to rethink it. The Judicial System there is no joke, and they will retire you. I stepped out of my house on the afternoon of New Year's Eve, 2003.

I had to make a quick stop at the supermarket to pick up something that I needed for my dinner. I detoured and ran into a clothing store. My friend, Jason, was with me on that day. He used to walk out of stores with bags of stolen clothes for me. I had promised Goldie, who was incarcerated, that I would send her some solid color shirts, so I figured I would grab a few to go. The undercover store detective, who watched us from a distance, thought otherwise. As we approached the exit, the security advanced on us. After that, everything else went into slow motion. Jason body slammed the security guard and we ran to my truck. As we rushed out of the parking lot, several witnesses got the description of my vehicle. I was so mad at Jason! All he had to do was give the bullshit shirts back and cooperate. All that drama could have been avoided. We were fugitives on the run. I knew the police would be arriving shortly. The type of neighborhood that I lived in didn't have any crime, so anything involving two blacks on the loose was going to be a major APB (All points bulletin). I wanted to get off the main road, so I swerved into an apartment complex and pulled into a parking slot. As I sat in the car, cursing him out for the dumb move he made, I heard the helicopters searching above. I knew that it was all over. Two seconds later, there were police surrounding us with their guns drawn. We were trapped! There were camera crews on the scene, and we made the news. I couldn't believe it! When we made it to court, it got worse. They charged us with robbery and kidnapping. The boosting turned into a robbery because he assaulted the security guard. When you touch a person and restrict their movement you can be charged you with kidnapping in the state of Ohio. It was a chumped up charge but they made it stick. I was devastated! Both of our bonds were one-hundred-thousand dollars. That was how I spent my 2003 New Year's Eve.

Queenie put up her house for my bond. She was always there to rescue me. I had made a promise to God that if he got me out of that jam that I was going to concentrate on my career, and get focused with my music. I kept that promise. I went in the studio and produced three mixtapes back. It was a way for me to vent about my life and I loved making songs.

I would go to the studio and record three songs a day. I created a crazy song catalog. My work ethics were just like my hustle ethics- nonstop delivery. I was obsessed with music and determined to get in the game. I didn't want to do another day in jail. Enough was enough! I hired the best attorney in the town. He was an old-timer who went golfing with the judge and the district attorney. After eight months of going back and forth to court, I got off with three years of probation, along with a three-thousand dollar fine. While I was out on bond, I caught another case in Nassau County, Long Island and did forty five days while I waited for Ohio to extradite me. At that point I realized that I had a severe money addiction akin to a drug addict. I needed help. I couldn't stop going in the stores and stealing. It was definitely starting to get to me. As you mature and see things differently, your priorities begin to change. I didn't care about being a fly girl. I wanted stability in my life. I didn't want to leave my daughter. My biggest fear was going to prison and leaving my baby girl. Eventually, my nightmare caught up with me.

Chapter Eight

Fee Fi Fo Fum

I went back to New York and focused on my music, Ohio had me shook and I wanted to be closer to the music industry. At that time New York was still running the rap game. I had to be close to the happenings. I needed a manager and my homie, Tut, hooked me up with his man, Rich, who had a few contacts in the business. I hollered at him and he started managing me. The biggest thing he did for me was getting Styles P to do a song with me. I've always admired the Lox. I followed their music and their D-Block movement. So, I was so excited when he made a phone call and the next thing I knew, we were at the infamous D-Block studio in Yonkers, New York. I met with Styles P and we vibed for a few. After that, I left him the track. I had already laid my verses and the hook. I am a wizard at coming up with hooks, and I had the perfect one for our song. I heard the hook in the melody of the music. Part of the hook goes like this 'Fee Fi Fo Fum, we're knocking down the doors here we come….' It's all about two giants, Styles P and Mack Mama, coming to do what we do slay the track. That is one of my favorite songs. Although it took him a while to get his verse back to us, it was nothing but fire and well worth the wait. His entire sixteen bars was about me, and that was his way of giving me his stamp of approval. It was a general saluting another general, and letting the streets know that I was certified. He is one of the hardest rappers in the game to me. His underground street credibility is unmatched, so that was big for me. I will always respect Styles P. for being a real dude. He didn't even charge me for the verse. Real stand up brother. I love the grittiness of this song. It always reminds me of back in the days when I was a gangstress.

I remember when Queenie and I used to hang out in the Nineties (that's an area in East Flatbush, Brooklyn). This is where some of the wildest Jamaicans and rude boys hung out. There would be shoot-outs almost every night. We loved the action and the excitement of it all. There were two brothers named Prince and Righteous, who were originally from Queens, but they owned a popular barber shop on 96th Street and Clarkson Ave in the Nineties. They were hood rich, and we loved them. They used to buy garbage bags full of stolen goods from us. It made boosting a lot more worthwhile when we had customers waiting with cash on the ready to buy everything. So, when Righteous, promised to pay us later for two minks, we let him owe us, figuring that he was good for the three grand. Besides, why would a brother named Righteous cheat us out of our money? He kept bullshitting around and didn't pay us our money. That was his first mistake. His second mistake was underestimating us. I was losing patience and wanted my money. That's when I put pressure on Queenie to step to him in the park, where he was playing basketball "Yo, there goes that bastard. Go ask him for our bread" I egged her on.

"Gurl, I hope this nicca' has this money" She said exasperated

"You! I'm not waiting anymore. We gon' have to do something to get our point across, cuz' homeboy trying to play us" I sulked, fed up. She walked over and asked him for our bread and I think he said something along the lines of the following: "Not now. When I get it, you'll get it. Beat it!" That was enough! When she came back to the car, I saw by the look on her face that it was ON! We went to see her man Sham God (R.I.P.) he was a hood "Arms Specialist", which meant he possessed all types of high-caliber weapons. He had no problem giving us an Uzi to take care of our problem. That's one thing I loved about Sham God; he was always there if we needed arsenals.

We waited to the wee hours of the morning and I drove to the barber shop. I was always the getaway driver on occasions like that. When we got in front of the barbershop, my partner, Queenie, let off a steady barrage of shots until the entire front window and inside mirrors were shattered, along with all the barber chairs being damaged in the process. Then I sped off as we heard the sirens approaching in the distance. We made a hell of a point. He would think twice before he beat another booster for their money. The damages to his shop had to total at least twenty grand, which is far more than he would have spent if he would have simply coughed up the three grand he owed us. Needless to say, we didn't have to worry about retaliation because Sham God had our backs. It always amazes me how much we managed to get away with, but sometimes things would catch up to us in the most unexpected ways. We had got caught boosting in the city a couple of weeks after the drive-by, and the cops found the spent shell castings from the Uzi in our vehicle. Back then we were so stupid. We had no idea that we had to clean up the shells after the shooting. We were just riding around with all that evidence. I had a small two-shooter .22 in my bra and, when the police found it, they branded us armed and dangerous. They couldn't believe that we'd been in a drive-by and I had the nerve to have a fire arm on my person. Like I've said, we were Original Bad Girls.

I know my mother is my angel because we were beefing with major drug dealers, and by all logic, we should be dead for the stunts we pulled. I am so blessed to be able to tell my story in a healthy state, free and unharmed. I'm not sitting in a wheel chair or a cell, and that is amazing. So, I figure that I am truly here for a reason. I have to touch all of the lost souls who are still in the streets (like I was), and let them know my story and see my change. If I can overcome all that I have been through and able to turn my life around, then any one can. I followed my dream for years and I am still a work in progress. However, if you're reading my autobiography, this is an accomplishment in itself.

Chapter Nine

EAST CRUNK

This song is the epitome of what every gangstress feels. It gets me hyped up every time I hear it. It is definitely the sound track of my adolescent years. I could have had it playing on repeat the night I finally got revenge on yet another girl that betrayed me. One thing about me that I have finally overcome is my bad temper. However, it was a point in my life when someone crossed me I went to any length to get them back. I was never a troublemaker nor a bully, but if you violated me, I had to get you back; especially when I was good to you. I was born on Valentine's day, so it's in my nature to love and not judge, but for some reason, people always mistook my kindness for weakness. That's when they would meet my other personality Mack Murder. There was no stopping me when she came out.

I am notorious for taking people in and trying to help them. This time it was another runaway who went to school with my sister. She was a pretty little girl named Iasia. One day, my sister brought her to meet me after some boys ran a train on her in the basement of one of their houses. She thought that she was pregnant and had a sexually transmitted disease. She was scared to tell her grandmother. She lived with her and would have gotten in trouble for cutting school. So, my sister asked me to let her stay with me for a while and, being the bleeding heart that I was, I invited her in with open arms. I took her to the clinic got her checked out, and basically, put her under my wing. She became like my little sister. We did everything together. I taught her how to get money and be fly. She never went back to her grandmother's place.

After about a year, we became so close that I thought she could be trusted. You can't trust anybody from the streets. You're never supposed to bite the hand that feeds you, and when I got bit, I bit back. I had to go do thirty days on Rikers Island, so I let her stay in my apartment with her boyfriend, whom I called my brother. I even hooked her up with another Brooklyn hustler called Greedy from Gates Ave. I wanted her to take Iasia out and make money; that way, she'll be able to look out for me while I was gone. Well, they decided that she shouldn't have to send me a third of what she was making (like we agreed on). I noticed that she wasn't sending me any money, so I started cursing her out on the phone. Things got bad and, when I came home, I was planning on knocking some sense into her head. I couldn't believe that she was dissing me for my associate; especially after I took her in and looked out for her like she was family. I had genuine love for that girl and she crossed me for another chick. Typical! It didn't stop there. She thought that she was leaving me to go work for Greedy permanently. Greedy was a freak and a coke head. I heard that she was freaking off with Iasia, and had her getting high. I was enraged! After all I did for her that was the thanks I got. She abandoned me for some head. She had no idea what loyalty meant, but I was going to teach her a lesson. I went and got Queenie and we went to Greedy's apartment, ready for war. I knocked on her door and she opened up nervously. She didn't want the drama and didn't waste any time calling the little traitor to the door. Greedy pushed her out in the hallway and closed her door on her. Smart move on her part, because I brought Queenie to jump on her, while I whooped the Benedict Arnold's ass. We didn't waste any time once we got the traitor in the hall way. "So, you thought you was gonna' diss me for that bitch?", I sputtered seething with fury.

"No" she whimpered.

"Yes, you did! You ungrateful bitch" **WHAP!** I hauled off and smacked her. After that it was on.

Queenie slammed her to the ground and kicked her viciously. Then we dragged her down the stairs, while still pummeling her with blows, and dumped her unceremoniously into the trunk of my car. We were crazy! Gates Avenue was packed with people. It was a summer night and everybody was outside, staring nosily. We took her to my crib and tied her to my bed, while continuing to smack her around. Queenie ended up leaving so I took over. She cried and begged for me to let her go use the bathroom. I should have let her urinate on herself, because as soon as I untied her, she bolted out the door. I chased her, but she got away. I was pissed but not really too concerned. I smoked a blunt and went to sleep, preparing to deal with finding her again the next day. Queenie told me to change my locks, but I paid it no mind. I should have listened. Yet, again I slept another snake. So, what happened? I got bit. I came home from hustling two days later and found a hanger swinging on my doorknob. She got me! The traitor did a full-fledged heist. She wiped me out. I'm talking about my televisions, stereo system, jewelry, clothes, purses and shoes. She hit me where it hurt. I kept her picture on my night stand for six months. Every time I looked at her picture, the pain was fresh, and I would plot my revenge. I had a hit out on her, but nobody had seen her. She was laying low. One night, I got a call that she was at the Empire Skating Rink, a popular rink in Brooklyn. I jumped up and headed to the rink. It was crowded that night. I had to play the wall and let everybody pass me. Finally, I spotted her and, sure enough, she was approaching me. Guess who she was with? Greedy! I had my razor in my mouth and I spit it out, getting ready to make my move. As soon as Greedy seen me, her eyes bugged out of her head. She signaled behind her as to tell me "There she goes." She sold her out! She knew somebody's ass was going to get touched, and she didn't want to be the victim. I let her pass and caught Iasia from behind as she passed me in the single file line. She never saw it coming. I had her in a choke hold and tore the flesh of her soft cheeks apart. I will never forget how it felt to slash her face. I was so happy to finally get her. I think that I might have shouted "**YES!**" She started screaming when the blood gushed from her face and I hauled ass out of the rink. Mission Accomplished!

That was the thing about the streets and the code I lived by. It was death before dishonor, and I honored that code. The funny thing is, I bumped into the traitor years later, and she actually apologized to "me". I was all ready to bang out when I saw her, but she quickly asked me could we talk. I was on guard, but I gave her a chance to talk. She told me how she knew she was wrong, and she wasn't mad about the scar on her face. I looked into her eyes and saw the truth. She was serious. Also, I saw the love. She actually still loved me. She even thanked me for all I had done for her. I was there for her when she couldn't turn to her own family, and she really appreciated me. She gave me a hug and I felt her sincerity. I was flabbergasted! I looked at her, and told her that she was still very pretty, and I'm glad that I didn't do any real damage to her face. She didn't have keloid skin, so the scar blended in smoothly with her creamy complexion. She was a red bone, with thick, long hair to cover the mark. I used to always tell her she was too pretty for the streets. So we laughed and reminisced for a few minutes and, after that, we parted our separate ways. That was the type of experiences I've had whenever I bump into people from my past. Either that or I will get the evil looks behind my back. One day, I bumped into the girl whose boyfriend I had shot in the stomach. I ran into her at a beauty parlor. I had forgot, that I shot her man, and actually had the balls to speak to her. She rolled her eyes so hard at me, they almost crossed. If I didn't have a reputation for being crazy, she probably would have tried to retaliate. Thank God she didn't, because I am a changed person. However, I am still obligated to defend myself. If you don't grow and mature, then you will be stuck in your ignorance. The only thing I'm stuck in is my youth. I have done so much time that I haven't aged in terms of my physical appearance. I take care of my body and watch the things that I put inside of it. I want to live and be healthy, so I can always be here for my daughter. I know how it feels to live your life without a mother. I don't ever want my baby to feel that pain.

Chapter Ten

WHAT CAN I DO?

This song is all about regrets. It was supposed to be for a soundtrack to a basketball movie that Dale Davis-from the Detroit Pistons- was producing. I had met him at one of my shows. His boy, Dave, had called him and told him about my performance. After that, he drove down in his limousine to meet me. He was looking for independent artists to be on his movie soundtrack, so we chopped it up about his project. It was about a basketball player who was accused of raping a groupie. It loosely followed the Kobe Bryant scandal. I was excited about the song. I did the first verse from the perspective of the psychopathic female who was obsessed with the player and was delusional about the whole situation. It was a different type of song. I had made the lyrics of the hook something everybody could relate to; those who were going through things in their lives.

The hook goes*: "What Can I Do to turn the hands back on time?/*

How can I go back to make things alright?/Guilty hearts makes the world tell lies/I Just can't figure out why/I just don't know what to do.."

I have so many regrets in my life. I can't turn the hands back on time, so I have to move forward and be a better me. The movie never came out. I just used the song for the soundtrack to my autobiography because it's so deep. It could be a Lady GaGa tune. The lyrics are poignant and my flow is very abstract.

The turning point in my life was my last and final bid, which I completed in 2009. Prior to that bid, I thought I was done with going to prison, but I had a rude awakening. Yet another person, I tried to help, snitched on me. For that, I received a five year sentence. She kept calling me, begging me to take her out to make some money, until I finally felt sorry for her and gave in. If I would have stayed focused on my career, it all could have been avoided. I had six mixtapes out and a heavy buzz in the underground circuit in New York. Everybody knew or heard of Mack Mama. My album was finished and I had at least fifty songs in my catalog ready to go. I had a promotional tour set-up, and I felt like I was finally going to do it. Then all of a sudden…BAM! I got bagged and my entire life seemed to float right before my eyes. I never got a chance to prepare myself for the bid.

In 2004, I took a woman named Pearl Dixon to Connecticut to make some money, using illegal credit cards. We went to several stores and successfully used the cards to purchase thousands of dollars in electronics and gift cards. At the last stop, which was Home Depot, she went in the store. After ten minutes, I saw the police enter the parking lot. I had my driver leave immediately. I already knew that the gig was up and they were there for her. I had tried to purchase some gift cards and was turned down because my identification didn't match the credit card I was using. so I left the store and waited for Pearl in the parking lot. I had pulled out the wrong I.D, which I'm never careless to that point. That was a sign that a fiasco was in the making. Pearl called my phone as I was en route to her house to drop off her share of the goods. She told me her bond was $100,000. I told her that if I had that type of money on hand I wouldn't have been out hustling and the best I could do is get her a lawyer. That wasn't good enough for her. As I was giving her things to her daughter-something that most hustlers wouldn't have done- she had her daughter write down the license plates to my Mercedes ML320. Pearl gave it to her arresting officer. Then she wrote a statement, informing him of every store we had been to, and how much I pay my workers for going into the stores and bring me merchandise. She painted the picture that I was the master mind and queenpin of a very lucrative operation. Now that I look back on it, I guess I was.

I had no idea that she had snitched on me, and, from that point, I didn't hear from her. I called her daughter on several occasions, trying to obtain information on her, so that I could send her some money, but she never returned my calls. I should have known something was up, but that thought never crossed my mind.

On April 6th 2005, I was stopped for a traffic violation in Massachusetts and arrested for a having a suspended license. I posted a hundred-dollar bond and, while I was waiting for a cab to pick me up from the station (my truck was towed earlier that day at the time of my arrest), I was rearrested and told that I had a warrant in Connecticut for sixty-five counts of credit card fraud. I was devastated! I didn't know what they were talking about. I swore that it was some kind of mistake. The police were very nice to me. Actually, they tried to help me, but it was out of their hands. I racked my brains as I sat in that freezing, cold cell, and couldn't figure out what I had done in Connecticut. After sitting there, shivering in absolute confusion, a light bulb went off in my head. Pearl! She had got knocked in Connecticut a year ago and she snitched on me. Well, I'll be damned. Ouch! I was bit once again.

When I went in front of the Judge, after being held in Massachusetts and extradited to Connecticut, he took one look at my lengthy rap sheet, and looked at me in disgust. I felt like a piece of shit. My dear friend, Poochie, was in the courtroom. She had traveled all the way from New York to support me and retrieve my truck from the tow company. I turned around and glanced in her direction. She gave me a sad smile of encouragement. The D.A. droned on and on about my history of warrants-for not showing up at court dates-and the numerous alias' I used, proving that I was a flight risk. The next statement he made almost caused me to pass out : "So your Honor, in light of her various felonies and out-of-state residency, it's our recommendation that she be held without bond...". I held my breath and, a tear ran down my face. I had never cried in court, but I knew that I was done, finished, finito`.

The Judge gave me a five- hundred- thousand dollar bond and scheduled my case for the next month. That was it. I was escorted back to the nasty dungeon, where the inmates were held underground beneath the court. It seemed like my life would never reach the surface. I couldn't wrap my head around a half a million dollar bond. I was hit! There was no way I could come up with that amount of money. I sat in that bull pen, surrounded by the lost souls. There were crack heads sleeping on the floor, while dope fiends vomiting in the steel bowl that we were supposed to share when we needed to relieve ourselves. I wanted to flush myself down that decrepit toilet.

I felt like my career was over. Any chances of my dreams coming true were diminishing, and it was my fault. I should have retired like I said I would. My mind kept rewinding back to the day I took Pearl out, and why she did the unthinkable. Snitching was punishable by death as far as I was concerned. It never failed. Every single person I tried to help in those streets had burned me. I wanted to kill her, because she took me from my daughter.

My Velvet was four years old when I left her. It destroyed me. It was history repeating itself. I was five years old when my mother went to jail and my godmother had to raised me. Now, Velvet's godmother, Queenie, would have to step up to the plate and take over for me. I wanted to crawl up in the corner of that cell and die. I couldn't stop the "what if's" They haunted me. What if I wouldn't have gone out that day I got arrested? What if I would have never went and picked Pearl up and took her hustling? What if I would have simply stopped hustling, maybe I wouldn't have been in that horrific situation. Initially, I felt that my music career would never happen. Once again, I had f**ked up and destroyed all chances of making it, but God had other plans for my life. Had I not got arrested, I would not have changed, and I certainly wouldn't have wrote my books : "Tales of an Original Bad Girl" and "Daisy Jones". Everything truly happens for a reason.

When I arrived at the York Correctional
Institution, which was affectionately called Niantic by
the old-timers who ran in and out of the Prison like it
was their time share, I was shocked. I was used to the
squat-and-cough deal the correction officers ran you
through during intake, but the two pairs of stiff denim
jeans, along with the two burgundy, raggedy t-shirts
second hand skips they made you wear on your feet
were crazy. They took all of my personal possessions
and stripped me of my dignity simultaneously. The
prison itself was wild due to being the only female
lock up in Connecticut, so everybody was thrown
together. I was housed with girls that were locked up
for murders and had life in prison. I couldn't believe it.
The correction officers were so mean and racist, not
only to the blacks but to the white girls, who they
looked down on as trash. Niantic was no joke. It was
the worst experience of my life. We were locked in our
cells eight hours a day.

Now, on the flip side, I have to say that it was a
much needed experience, because it changed me in so
many ways. The first Sunday of my incarceration, I
went to church and heard this woman speak. She was a
visiting evangelist. Her testimony was about how she
used to be in Niantic, and she was a recovering crack
addict. She gave her life to Jesus Christ. He forgave
her for all of her sins, which meant that she was saved.
That message touched my soul and I cried like a baby.
Every layer of hate and anger peeled off of me in that

small area we sat in and had church. I cried out to God to forgive me for all of my sins, and I felt a weight lifted off of my shoulders. I surrendered to Jesus Christ that day and I was serious. I went back to my cell and cut off all my hair. I wanted a new beginning. I wanted to shave off my vanity, so that I wouldn't attract any attention from the girls. That was my biggest sin; my lust for women. When I cut my hair, I had cut off Mack Mama and had become Christian Coco. I read my bible all day and prayed for my life. I didn't socialize with anyone but the few ladies who were saved and read their bibles. We had prayer groups and bible study sessions on the tier. I felt a sense of peace. My family couldn't believe the new me, and were skeptical about my change.

I was put to the test in a major way. I was told to move to another area in the prison, so I packed up my belongings and reported to my new cell. When the door buzzed open, I locked eyes with Pearl. I hadn't seen her since I'd arrived and didn't know how I would handle it. So, imagine how I felt when I met my new Bunkie, and it was the person who was responsible for me being in prison. I was shocked. Her face just fell. She looked like she had seen a ghost. I looked at her and felt pity. I told her "Pearl I am saved. I forgive you." She burst out crying. Then she hugged me, telling me how sorry she was. That experience was the turning point in my growth and development. As you know, from reading my memoirs, that if I didn't have God in my life, I would still be in prison for seriously hurting that woman in that cell.

She was saved, too. So we read our bibles together and we prayed. She received two years for giving me up, but there was another case in New Jersey that she had to do four years on. All crimes were paid eventually. She told on me, but still had to pay her debt to society. I joined the choir in church and started writing gospel rap and songs. I seriously considered going to college for Theological Studies and becoming a pastor. I went to a three day, spiritual retreat called Kairos. It was an awesome program ran by women of the cloth that came in from the outside to show us some much needed love. They helped us learn to forgive and love ourselves, others and God. I couldn't believe the amount of hate that I had stored inside of me, and I let it all go on that retreat. It felt good to let go of all that bitterness I've had stored inside of me for so many years. I wrote my ex-husband a letter and told him that I forgave him for all the physical and emotional abuse he'd put me through. He never responded, but it felt good to release myself from the burden of hate that I felt for him.

When my family heard that Pearl was my cell mate, and we were cool, they knew that I was serious about my new found religion. I was Christian Coco for eighteen months until Satan decided that he wanted me back.

I had become very depressed from missing my daughter. So, I had made a decision that I didn't want her to visit me in jail, but it was getting to me. Satan knew how to come at me, so he sent a female to lure me back into his lair. She started writing me and going hard, trying to get me. I began liking the attention and slowly stopped reading my bible, the guilt of my attraction to this girl made me stop going to bible study and my prayer groups. I had started writing her back and, before I knew what happened, my lust for women came rushing back like a flood. She wanted to please me, so I finally gave in to my desires. I felt so ashamed that I had let God and my sisters in Christ down that I literally left the whole Christian Coco personality alone. I told everybody to call me Mack Mama because Christian Coco was gone.

Everybody thought I was nuts. I had completely flipped. I had since moved from the cell with Pearl and, when I saw her again, she was in for a shock. I told her I was mad all over again, thinking about how she got me locked up, and took me from my daughter. I wanted to flip on her. Satan had won. He lied dormant, waiting to strike and attack when I was at my lowest, most vulnerable point. When slipped into a depressive state, I had lost faith in God's word, and Satan caught me slipping. As of this writing, I am still a back slider in terms of my commitment to Jesus Christ, but in the eyes of my lord and savior, I am still his child. He patiently awaits my return back to his throne. I know that I have a calling in my life and I am highly favored by the Lord. I will be back!

Chapter Eleven

DANCE ON

I was moved to the east side of the prison, which held the inmates who were considered minimum risk and had done a large percentage of their sentence. I had done two-and-a-half years and, by right, I should have been home because I had a nonviolent crime. However, I had some fights and a physical altercation with a C.O., so I got hit at the parole board. When I turned back to my old self, all of the anger returned. I had zero tolerance for the bullshit that went on in that prison. To be honest, it all stemmed from the "bulldaggin". I was fighting over the girl I was with simply because other females were jealous and wanted to be with her. She had a fan club, but she wasn't worth all the drama. She was a freak and a big flirt. So, I was involved in nonsense that I wasn't used to, and totally out of my character. I should have been focused on my freedom, but I slipped and got lost in that ignorant mindset. That can easily happen when you're surrounded by that much negativity. Birds of the same feather flock together, and when you sleep with dogs, you wake up with fleas. I grew up listening to the wise adages of my deceased, sweet godmother. She had a saying for every situation and those are my favorites.

I actually did fifty four days in segregation behind shoving a correction officer out of the way to get to the freak I was with. I found out that she was creeping on me and wanted to rip her head off. While I was in segregation, I found a peace of mind. It was serene. I was in the cell by myself and no one bothered me. I spent my days writing and creating new songs that I would perform over and over again for my audience. The seven other inmates that filled the cells on the tier were all I had to entertain. They appreciated me spitting a hundred bars and singing at the top of my lungs like I was a contestant on American Idol. I would look in the plastic tin foil, which served as a mirror in my cell, and imagined that I was on stage. I used my imagination and transported myself out of that tiny cell and felt the heat from the spot light. I heard the roar of approval from the crowd and my heart would soar. I couldn't wait to get home. I would practice giving interviews, and I actually gave a lot of girls in that prison my autographed head shot pictures that I had my family send in. I always carried myself like a star. I wrote a song once inspired by a C.O. who laughed at me when I told her that I was going to be a star.

FAMOUS IN MY MIND

Hook:

I'm Famous in my mind. If you tell me I'm not, you're wasting your time....

I'm famous in my heart. I'm a keep on striving even though it gets hard....

Verse 1:

Never let my spirit's sink, no matter what they think.   I live for the fame everybody knows my name.....

I'm rising to the top and I'm never gonna' stop.......

(repeat hook)

Verse2:

Don't criticize my work I got what it takes....

My destiny is set all I need is faith.....

I keep my head held high....

Till I reach the sky.....

(repeat hook)

Verse 3:

I'm a mega superstar, traveling 'round the world….

Flying very far since a little girl….

My dreams my parachute, I land on my feet…

If you feel the way I feel, sing this song with me….

(repeat hook)

"I'M FAMOUS IN MY MIND. IF YOU TELL ME I'M NOT, YOU'RE WASTING YOUR TIME…

I'M FAMOUS IN MY HEART. I'M A KEEP ON STRIVING EVEN THOUGH IT GET'S HARD…

When she came back around to do her rounds, I had that song ready for her butt. After I finished singing to her, she got such a kick out of me that every time I saw her, wherever I was in the prison, she would tell me to sing that song for other officers. She couldn't believe that I wrote that song just because she kept telling me I wasn't a star. As long as I think it, believe it and feel it, I am "IT". I am a Star! I encourage everybody to think that way about themselves no matter what your circumstances are. That type of self-confidence is the only way to achieve success. The measure of success is happiness and being content in your life. That's all I want. Oh!... And lot's of **MONEY!** (*wink)

I used to go outside for my hour of recreation handcuffed, but that didn't stop me from jogging and rapping simultaneously to build endurance and stamina when I performed. Everything I did was in preparation for my career. I had plenty of time to focus and think about my mistakes, I used all of my solitude to create and plan my future. Everything I said I was going to do once I regained my freedom, I am doing. That is an accomplishment in itself, and I must say I am very proud of myself.

When I came out of segregation and returned to population, I was ready to go home. I had finally calmed down and had enough. I wanted out! My security level had gone down from a "four" to a "one" and I landed the best job on the compound. I worked off-grounds and was allowed to leave the facility without being hand cuffed. Along with a crew of three other women, I was selected to clean different off-ground sites like the local Fire Department or Camp grounds. The civilians treated us so nice, and I finally felt like I regained my respect. At no time did I feel like a lowly inmate. The correction officer I worked for named Ms. Rushford, treated us like real employees. She was a sweetheart and the perks of the job were awesome (real food). I loved it when we went to the Camp Ground. They had a chef on grounds, and we had gourmet lunches. The work was hard but I enjoyed it. It gave me a sense of accomplishment. I would clean four cabins from top to bottom by myself.

I would have never imagined working a job like that when I was home. I have always been a boss, and never would have had to clean toilets and scrub floors on my knees. Prison will humble you and make you grateful for the small things in life. I got paid $1.75 a day, which was nothing, but the rewards were great for me. I can clean a bathroom like nobody's business (lol).

I used to tell my bunkies that I was going home to make it big, and I would perform my songs for them. I threw parties in my dorm and organized talent shows. I always knew how to make people feel good. Nothing makes me feel better than being the center of attention and doing my thing. I made sexy costumes and did my hair and makeup like I was really on stage. With my brush as my microphone, I would strut all over my room, while singing and rapping my heart out. I spent a lot of time working out and encouraging the women that I lived around to work out with me. I didn't eat any of the junk food that they sold on commissary, nor did I eat red meat, so I survived off of canned food. I thank God that I was blessed my entire bid with money, plus I had all the necessities that I needed to do my time comfortably. I relied on my best friends, Poochie and Queenie, for my steady income. In addition, my grandmother would send me what she could. At that time, my girlfriend who I called Mafia looked out for me so good that I was able to send my daughter five-hundred for Christmas in 2007. I was truly blessed. I always say when your good to folks, folks are good to you. My sister put all my clothes and belongings in storage and made sure she never missed a payment. I managed to come home to all my possessions, which is practically unheard of after doing a long bid. I am so grateful. My main goal was to keep my body sexy, so I would have the whole package. It's so important for me to have the talent and the "look". My image is so natural because I have always been a fly girl. I style myself and do my own hair and makeup, so I don't have to rely on anyone to create my image. I am Mack Mama from the tip of my nose to the end of my toes. It's pure mackiness. First and foremost, I am a business woman, so I treat myself as a brand. I promote Mack Mama the product.

My song Dance On was inspired by my sex-sells series, XXX rated mixtape. That is the erotic side of me, my mackalicious personality. It came about because I was too hard-core on my prior mixtapes. I sounded too angry and way too grimey on my underground mixtapes, and actually had guys beg me to lighten it up and spit some sexy lyrics. I thought about it and decided that they were right. I am sexy and pretty. I could easily pull off the XXX Rated thing, but I wasn't going to talk about the regular, raunchy shit that Lil' Kim was known to rap about. I rap about what a man has to do to and for me. Most guys like to call me a gold digger, but I prefer Mack Mama. I am a female P.I.M.P (Pay Interest on MY

P***y) because I refuse to give up my most prized possession for free anymore; especially since I have the worst luck with men. I might as well get paid for the pain and suffering that comes with the relationship. If I sound bitter, I don't mean to be that way. I'm just speaking from my past horror stories that I have shared with you. I guess that's why I enjoy being with a woman. I have much better luck with the same sex. It's as simple as that. Men always tell me they won't hurt me, and I know that some of them mean well, but I am not ready to take that chance. I'd rather focus on my career and give myself through my music. My male fans love me and think that I'm a total freak because of my XXX Rated mix Cd.

Well the truth is that is only my mackalicious persona. It lives inside of me, but by no means am I a raving nympho who wants to get laid and paid. I channeled my inner Madame for that entire cd, and I wanted to have fun and represent all the exotic dancers who sell sex fantasies. Those ladies "get it". To all the young girls- that includes my own daughter who will read my autobiography when she turns thirteen. Do not sell yourself cheap! So many girls are screwing around without protection, while unable to get a meal out of the guy. Not only are you risking your life, but no man will respect anything that's not protected. He will go in raw and treat your body like a dumping ground. Leaving a baby or a disease if he pleases. He certainly won't treat you like a queen if you're acting like a whore. I'm going to tell you like this, a man won't give you anything if he already got it for free. Hold on to your prize and make him earn the privilege of making love to you. I have a six-month rule that will prove if he really likes you. If he will wait and spend his money, trying to get you, while treating you like his Queen, then he is the one. If he can't wait tell him to SKATE! Or even better than that, virgins ROCK!!! (Velvet that is for you baby, make your mama proud. I want to live vicariously through you. Everything I did wrong, you can do right. I love you, baby.) AND YOU BETTER BE THIRTEEN IF YOU'RE READING THIS. OR ELSE!... ☺

Chapter Twelve

WORK YA

I missed my daughter to the point where I was getting physically ill from thinking about her so much. I wrote every mother and child halfway house in Connecticut, trying to get any one of them to accept me into their program. I wanted to be with her immediately, and I was sick and tired of prison it had been 3 ½ years and I was ready to go home. Velvet was also very anxious to see me. At the time, she was seven, and I had finally let her see her father. She was happy but wanted both of us back in her life, I knew that would never happen as a family unit, but I was determined to be cordial to her dad so she would be happy. Finally on September 12th 2008 I was picked up by the Neon Mother and Child program. I was deliriously happy and couldn't wait to see my daughter. I had a shrine of her pictures surrounding me the entire time I was incarcerated, and I had only seen her on six visits. I finally gave in and allowed my family to bring her to see me but she lived in Ohio, which was really too far for frequent visits. So, I was hyperventilating from anticipation the thought of finally holding my child again.

The halfway house was an apartment building that held six, two-bedroom apartments, with four girls in each apartment. I had my own room that I shared with my daughter, and there were two other ladies in the apartment with us. Compared to the cell that I had lived in for so long, it felt like a mansion. The funny thing was, there was only one other child in the building, and she was a baby so Velvet had no one to play with. I couldn't understand why there were so many women sitting in jail, waiting for a mother-and-child program for the purpose of reuniting with their children. Yet, the program was full of women that didn't even have kids. What a waste! The system never gets it right. Just like there is no program for people that suffer from money addiction like me. They have all types of drug programs that the court recognizes as alternatives to incarceration, but nothing for boosters, check writers, credit card fraud, or people that pick pockets. We have serious problems controlling our addiction, and we relapse and have triggers just like drug addicts and alcoholics. How else can you explain why we keep going to prison for the same thing and can't stop chasing money? We ruin our lives by our destructive behavior and deserve the same sympathy from the courts as drug addicts. When I get into position to be heard, I swear I am going to fight for a Money Addiction program in every State in the U.S.

My daughter and I spent our days getting to know each other and enjoying each other's company. It was a struggle at times for me to discipline her whenever she'd done wrong, because she thinks I am her home girl. (Because I'm so cool), however; when it's time to listen, I demand my respect. I remember I had to teach her a lesson about loyalty. I had snuck a cell phone in my room. We weren't allowed to have them in the halfway house, but I needed my phone (it was my office). The Internet on the touch-tone phones fascinated me, and I quickly adapted to the new technology. Well, one day my daughter saw me hiding the phone and realized that I shouldn't have it. So being the Lil' Mack that she is, she'd decided to use that against me when I reprimanded her about something. She actually said to me, "I'm going downstairs and tell them about your phone." I was in shock. I was so mad at her, because that was wrong on so many levels. How you going to snitch on your own mama!? She had to get a quick lecture about loyalty. I made her realize that if she was to let her anger make her do something that could get me sent back to prison, she would regret it, but it would be too late. I later realized that by her seeing me hide that cell phone, I was inadvertently teaching her how to be sneaky. I regret that one, but as I always say, I'm a work in progress. One of the things I love about my daughter and my relationship is that I don't sugar coat anything with her and she understands. She apologized and we discussed our loyalty to each other. Then we pinky-swore that no matter how mad we got at each other, we would always have each other's back.

I went through so much drama in that halfway house with the director of the program. She was a hater and didn't like me. I wasn't letting her talk to me any kind of way like the other girls did, and wasn't intimidated by her in the least. I called her out for stealing our supplies and using the money for our groceries for her personal use. She had been doing it for years, and could have continued had she not picked me to mess with. When you do dirt you can't act like your shit doesn't stink. She started harassing me as soon as she seen who I really was. Most of the women who come to that program need the secondhand clothes that they provided, because they don't have any real support from their families. She treated them like derelicts. I was from out of town, so she had no idea who I had in my corner. When my packages started coming every other day and my people started flooding me with money, she got real jealous. It was sad. Instead of being happy to see I had support from the outside, she began to pick at me. Everything was a problem. She claimed that I had too many clothes, too much jewelry, and too much money in my account. The last straw was that she tried to block my daughter from coming to stay with me; simply because I had gave temporary custody of her to my sister while I was incarcerated. I fought hard for my baby to get there and was determined to get the director off of my back. What better way than to expose her for the sneaky, illegal shit she was doing. One thing I've learned from going to prison is the pen is mightier than a sword. I used to write up any C.O. who messed with me, and she was no different. As long as you know the correct policy and procedure, while going through the proper chain of command, you will get favorable results (most of the time). She had no idea who she was messing with. As a result of writing her superiors, we had a meeting with all the important people in the Neon Organization. I had her so frazzled that she was actually screaming at me during the meeting. She made herself look so ignorant, while I spoke very eloquently and stated my points clearly and articulately. I was aiming to get her fired, but she managed to cover her tracks in regards to the stealing she was doing. What I got from that meeting was a new level of respect. The entire house knew I went up against the director of the program and didn't get sent back to prison. I actually exposed her pilfering ways and got away with it. That was a victory in itself. Needless to say, she left me alone. After that, I was able to go and come in peace. I didn't want my daughter to feel like she was a prisoner, so one of my issues was being allowed to take her to the mall and the library at will. After that, we were out damn near every day. Most of the counselors there loved me, and I stop by and visit them until this day. I am legendary in that place. I am the only woman that went to bat against the powers that be and got results.

I will never forget that place because I met my angel in there. Kenya "Sparkles" Williams. Coincidently, we have the same last name, so I know it was meant for us to be in each other's lives. She worked for a government funded program called ATR, which helps inmates with clothing and transportation funds to go job hunting. She would come to the house on a certain day of the week and hold group meetings and do intake on the new girls. When I first met Sparkles I was fresh off the bus, suited in my gray jail sweatpants. I looked a hot mess, but I still had my New York swag. The girls told me that Kenya was giving out gift cards to go shopping for cosmetics and I wanted in on that. She was so nice to me. When I told her that I was a rapper from New York that piqued her interest. I wanted to impress her, so I started rapping. Then I gave her my myspace info, so that she could check me out and see that I was official. Thanks to my friend Ndy, I had a myspace page while I was incarcerated. He would pretend he was me, while keeping my music and pictures popping on there. I love him for that. I also love him for bringing my daughter up to see me whenever she came to New York.

Kenya was the flyest person I had seen since I've been in Connecticut and I wanted her on my team. I knew that I had stay in Connecticut, since I had a year left on parole. I would need someone who knew the town and could assist me in finding a crib. That way, I could get out of the halfway house. She was a blessing from God. She asked me what I needed and I told her a flat iron. All I wanted was to do my hair nice for my visit. The next day, she brought me two bags full of cosmetics and hair products, along with a nice flat iron. I was impressed that she spent her own money to purchase the stuff. She was a class act. She didn't know me from Adam, but went all out for me. I was so grateful. It's hard to find people with that type of giving spirit nowadays, and that is how I am, so I hold on to good finds like that. She became my best friend. She eventually gave up her job when the hating director of the program gave her an ultimatum. She submitted the forms to visit me on her off days, but she was told it was a conflict of interest, so she quit that job. To this day, I think that was the kindest thing someone has ever done for me. Of course, she had other sources of income, but to give up her job just so she could visit me, and make sure I was straight was deep. She made a good investment because I give her my all. She will be straight for as long as I am breathing. Loyalty! I say no more.

She hooked me up with a cute, three-bedroom apartment in her building when it was time for me to leave, so I didn't have to go through the hassle of looking for a place. Everything just fell into my lap. Queenie sent me a beautiful living room, dining room and bedroom set; therefore, I was straight on the furniture. The day I came home, Sparkles surprised me by arranging all my furniture. She also filled my refrigerator and cabinets with food for me and Velvet. She is a jewel that's why I call her Sparkles. Those are the types of people I have in my life. I don't have many friends, but the few that I have are life long and loyal.

I have developed into an antisocial person from being in prison so long. I have a distrust of women due to the jealousy and cattiness I was surrounded by in prison. Those experiences made me look at females in a different light. I never understood why women act like that at times. I compare my mentality to that of a male, because I can't identify with how the average female thinks. When I see a woman looking nice, I compliment the sister. When I see a lady doing her thing, I salute her for it. I have never been an envious person. If women stopped hating on each other, and used that energy to uplift each other, we would be unstoppable. Look at the state of the females in the Industry. It has been the same names for decades. Why is that? That is because females who are in position to bring other talented sisters in the door just don't do it. When, I get into a power position, I will make sure, that I see my dream of an all-female rap group come to fruition. I want us to be like a female Wu-tang, but we'll be reppin' O.B.G.'s. If I have my way, at least twenty, talented ladies will breathe some much needed estrogen in the music industry. For now, I'm happy that Nicki Minaj is bringing the female emcee back (when she is not a pop singer), I wanted to be the first, but she beat me to it. I'm not mad. I salute her success. She has a different following than I do. Like she said, she's for the "Youth dem" (in her Trinidadian accent). I am more for the grown and sexy audience, but that's good, because we need diversity in the game. So many people hate on that girl, but I personally knew that she would blow up. She has the whole package and, without a doubt, she is the future of hip-hop. I paid a tribute to her by making a mix cd called "Mack-N-Minaj". I figured that two five-star chicks on one Cd would be great, plus it would introduce me to her fan base. I used her underground music (before she switched up her style) combined with my hard-core, underground songs. I love when she spit the songs that I can relate to, because I am definitely not a Barbie. I have certain songs where I am expressive, but I'm more sexy than animated on a track. However, homegirl is talented, and I love watching her. She's very entertaining. I would love to work with her and do a song together. That would be sexy. People say that she stole Lil' Kim's style, but I think she took it and made it better. Besides, Lil' Kim wasn't using it anymore. No one gets mad at the pop stars that wear bleached, blonde hair and imitate Marilyn Monroe.

It's typical for females in the industry to go at each other, and I only hope that when I enter the game, nobody comes at me, because I want peace. I did all of my dirt in the streets and paid my dues. I damn sure don't want to get in the game and beef with individuals, because I know how Mack Murder can get and she is a beast! If someone messes with Mack Mama she will be very upset. I am putting it out there now. I want to do collaborations with Nicki Minaj, Eve, Trina, Shawna, Missy, and my all-time favorite emcee Dabrat. I also have my own all-female group called O.B.G's which consists of Lace Stonze and Bliss Boogie a.k.a Malorie Knox. We are definitely coming! I live for female emcees, and I would rather join forces than divide and conquer.

I worked two legitimate jobs in my life. Both were when I came home from my final bid in 2008. The first one was a ninety-day gig at a work-training program that hired me from the halfway house. It was a factory job and I enjoyed it. I loved the nuns who ran the program, and thank them for that opportunity. Sister Marie founded the program called "IN THE MAKING", to help women like me who had no work experience and adversities like felonies on our records. Those obstacles usually ostracize ex-cons from the work force. I commend "IN THE MAKING" for giving me an opportunity to work. I am a perfectionist, and I give my all to whatever I do. They hated to see me go, but the program is designed to rotate every ninety days, so everybody can get a shot.

I found my second job on my own. It was telemarketing and I hated it. I had to set up bookings over the phone for Kirby vacuum cleaners. First of all, we're in a recession, so who has money for a thousand dollar vacuum? You can imagine how many times I've had the phone slammed down in my ear, but, surprisingly, I became pretty good at convincing people to hear me out. I became one of the top bookers. I have the gift of gab. It's a New York thing. We are known as fast talkers. I didn't like the hours that I was working. Split shifts and weekends for two hundred dollars weekly was Insane! I hardly saw my daughter. It wasn't worth it, so I quit that job. That was the extent of my adventures in the work force. I had decided I could make money off of what I did best, which was performing.

My first party was in a tiny club in a little town in Connecticut called Ansonia. I made that club live as hell that night. I even had a camera crew film the party. They thought I was doing a reality show. Those people had never seen anything like it. I hosted the party and I performed. I had a booty-shaking contest, which had the chicks battling with their butts for a fifty dollar prize. It was hilarious. Then I got up on a table and performed "Dance On". It was outrageous. I had the DJ play some of my songs. The song "Work Ya" was a big hit. It is one of my favorite party tunes. I recorded it with a Jamaican artist from Brooklyn named Plucky Ranks. It's hilarious. We go back and forth on why I think he should try oral sex and his reasons for not wanting to bless me with the treat.

I love performing, and I come alive in front of an audience. On the contrary, I'm so laid-back and reclusive when I'm off stage. That is from getting bitten too many times. For that reason, I don't trust human beings; they are way too complex for me to figure out. When you're a new artist, you have to let the audience know who you are instead of just getting up there and they have no idea who they are watching. People leave my show feeling like they knew me for years and I am their favorite artist.

I love being Mack Mama. It is who I was born to be. I took a leap of faith when I quit my job and decided to start hosting my own parties, but it worked. I made money doing what I loved to do. The only setback was the location wasn't ideal. The party goers in New Haven, Connecticut are cheap. It is unbelievable, but they only pay ten dollars to get into a club. I have seen folks pay up to a hundred dollars or more to get into a hot club, so I was boggled. I was only making a paltry two to three-hundred dollars at the door. After I spent two hundred on flyers to promote the event, I barely broke even. I had a couple of clubs agree to let me host certain nights, and I would create the theme for that night like Mack Mama's Paradise. Then I started bringing in the strippers and it would get real raunchy. However, the money wasn't right, so I ended the shows. My girls weren't getting paid enough for all the tricks those cheap guys wanted them to perform. So, I decided to take a break and devise another plan to make money, while getting my brand and music out there.

I started a viral campaign. I went hard on all the social networking sites. I released my album on iTunes, amazon.com and reverbnation.com/mackmama. I had my website designed and uploaded all my mixtapes to music sharing sites like datpiff.com and youtube.com. I filmed my parties and uploaded the footage. Then I began to get the Mack Mama brand out there. I received so much positive feedback and made a lot of connections. The funny thing was, I wanted to test the "sex sells" theory, so I released my newly revised XXX Rated music. Then I did a sexy photo shoot and posted the pics on my facebook fan page. I went from six hundred friends to five thousand in two weeks. I was amazed. Men are my biggest fans, and that is solely based on my image. I really want to reach women who can relate to what I'm talking about on so many levels; whether their hustlers, victims of abuse, or just the underdogs in life who want their time to shine. Let's not forget the exotic dancers that just want to get paid for their work. It's so hard to get a job these days, and these bold women are doing what they have to do to survive. I give a special shout out to those ladies, because it's hard to do all that degrading shit, while dudes wants to slow feed them with dollars all night. I Love exotic dancers and I dedicated my XXX Rated mixtape to them. I personally will go broke making it rain on dancers. I feel their pain. It takes guts and a hell of an imagination to do what those ladies do. I wish I had the patience to be an exotic dancer. I would be paid with my body and sex appeal. People always think I am a stripper. I just don't have the patience to do all of those tricks. Then I'm spinning on the pole all night while a nicca' 'dollaring me to death. I know that I would mess around and rob his ass. I have zero tolerance for a cheap man.

Chapter Thirteen

ALL I WANNA KNOW?

I am hurting as I write this, because I am currently dealing with a very stressful situation, which stems from me opening up my bleeding heart yet again. I always want to help, but I realize that humans have gone bad... plain and simple. It's only a few good ones left. I did a lot of treacherous shit in my life, and I'm nowhere near perfect, but I am a good person and I have a pure heart. I call myself an Original Bad Girl due to my past lifestyle, along with the trials and tribulations I've went through because of my bad choices, but when you know better you do better. I have a tattoo on my lower back that depicts the struggle I go through every day. There are flames flickering underneath my Angel wings with O.B.G. in the center of the halo. I am a lost soul trying to be an angel, trying desperately to be the human that God wants me to be. But, that 'ole Satan is constantly waiting for me to slip up and fall back into my old ways. If I do, the eternal flames of hell will be waiting

With that being said here is my last tale. It is what I am going through at the time of this writing. I want to prefix this by letting my darling readers know that if by chance I don't make it out of this situation due to life imprisonment or possibly death, that I am trying with all my power to do the right thing. I have to handle this situation like society dictates that I should, and how Jesus Christ would have handled it, lawfully and compassionately. It is hard because I am a struggling O.B.G. and violence usually fixed all the foul humans that have crossed me. I have surely changed, so I handle things much differently, now.

The title of the song that matches this situation is called "All I Wanna' Know". It's about a man wanting to know if I want to be with him, but I have my guards up due to all of my past drama with relationships. What I am about to share has nothing to do with the above mentioned song. All I 'wanna' know is why the hell is my so-called godson stalking me? He stated that he wants me to die slowly and painfully because I deserve it. I promise you that I did nothing to this boy other than looked out for him and tried to help. God knows that I shouldn't have had anything to do with him because of what his uncle, Crax, did to me. All I wanted to do was merely say **"hi"**.

I received a call one day from my father. He asked me did I want Crax's mother to have my number. She had called him and wanted to speak to me. I deliberated for a minute and decided against my better judgment that he could give it to her. I had remembered how good she had treated me and my daughter. I didn't want to diss her based on what her son had done, so I took her number. That was a mistake.

When I called her we had a nice conversation. I asked about my godson, which is Crax's nephew. She went on to vent to me about how she had put him out because he was lazy and didn't do anything but stay on the computer all day. He had been stabbed and wouldn't tell on his attackers, and she was scared for his life. I gave him a call to see how he was doing and we were both happy to hear from each other. He told me his "sob story". I'm a sucker for a good sob story. He said he was staying at his mother's friend's apartment, but she was kicking him out and he was heading to a shelter. He was so excited to speak to me and immediately started telling me how talented he was with making beats. He wanted to help me with my music so I wouldn't have to spend money in the studio for engineering or production. He said all I needed was to buy him a program for his computer called Protools and we would be all set. He was always a computer geek, so I considered what he said and decided I wouldn't let that type of talent go to waste in a shelter.

I told him that I would let him stay with me. That was the second worst mistake. I hadn't seen this boy since he was sixteen, and I was with his uncle. Now he was a twenty-two year old man. He had grown up physically, but mentally he was still a little boy. When I went to pick him up, he looked like a Grisly bear. He had a rough-looking beard and his skin was the color of midnight. He was dressed in all black, which made him look very menacing. That should have been my first sign. But when he hugged me and I began talking to him, he was my old godson (just in a bigger package). I asked him about his life, and why he was in such a rut. That's when he shared his grief about his mother. She was very close to me. We met in prison and went on to become good friends.

His uncle, Crax was locked up, while his father had moved out of town to deal with his own addictions and his other family. He was on his own and had nothing but his Social Security check that he received monthly. That sealed the deal. I needed that assistance and decided he would be an asset to my career and not a liability, so it could work. He went to a technical school for audio and digital production, so he was trained to engineer and produce music. I was going to get him all the programs and equipment that he needed to begin setting up my in-house studio. I even gave him a laptop off the rip because that's how I do things. I love to make my love ones happy, and he was so miserable.

I even took him shopping for a few outfits, as well. It was his birthday and the kid didn't have anything but a small suitcase with more black hoodies and a few jeans. I felt so sorry for him and wanted to make him feel good. I liked to see his face light up like it was Christmas when we went to restaurants like Red Lobsters. That was my seafood McDonald's but for him it was like a five-star restaurant.

After seven days, I was ready for him to go. He was sloppy, lazy, and didn't like to put the toilet bowl seat down, which drove me bonkers. I couldn't believe he was a grown man. He acted like a teenager, and had no home training. Everything he did seemed to annoy me. I finally lost it when I noticed droplets of piss on my bathroom floor. I found myself becoming stressed out, and I didn't like it. I still gave him the benefit of the doubt because of his talent. I didn't want to turn my back on him like he thought his family did, but I saw what his grandmother was talking about, which explained why he was on his way to the shelter. That was the first strike.

I told him to start promoting my music on the internet, but I discovered that instead of doing what I needed done, he was watching porn all night. He was addicted to every porn site on the web and knew all of the porn stars. He started telling me about how he didn't want a girlfriend because he was not well-endowed and didn't want to be rejected, so he lived in his virtual world.

He had his pick of woman with the click of a button. He also admitted that he would masturbate daily in my shower to relieve himself. I didn't take that information kindly. I went off about that. I started seeing a sick side of him that disturbed me, and it was strike two.

Strike three was the deal breaker. My friend, Mighty dropped by to take me on a date and, while I entertained him, this psycho starts tripping. He started blasting one of Lil Wayne's rock songs, the one with Eminem where he says, "I'm gonna' pick up the world and drop it on your f***ing head" I couldn't believe he had my theater system on level twenty. My walls were vibrating. When I opened my door to tear him a new asshole, this mother sucker was in the pitch dark, pacing back in forth in my living room with a knife in his hand. I lost it for real: **"WHAT THE F**K IS YOUR MALFUNCTION?"** I pulled him down the hallway into my kitchen and cursed him out in a furious whisper. I didn't want Mighty to hear me and realize that he had that knife, because he would have shot him on the spot. "What are you doing!!? Why do you have that knife? And what's with that music blaring in here?"

He slurred out the following response : "I don't want no nigga' in here while I'm here. That's word to my mother, I will kill that 'nigga! I'm your pit bull. 'Aint nobody gonna' have you while I'm in this mother f***er!" By then, I realized that he was drunk, and the crazed look in his eyes told me that he was serious as cancer. I managed to calm him down. Then I hurried back to my friend, and we left out of there. I laughed the situation off as being nothing. I told Mighty that my crazy godson was drunk and loved Lil' Wayne and Rock music. We laughed about it and enjoyed the rest of our nigh. However, I was seething in the back of my mind, and couldn't wait to get his ass out of my house.

The next day, I told him that he had to leave. He pleaded and apologized, but that was the straw that broke the camel's back. I wasn't budging. I was going to let him go to Queenie's building in Ohio to start setting up my studio, but that deal was off. I wanted no parts of his crazy ass. He reminded me of his uncle, Crax, when he started going off the deep end on those drugs. The whole family was cookoo for coco puffs, and I was just as nuts for dealing with them. I was done! The bleeding heart shit had to stop. It was getting dangerous. He wrote me a love letter, expressing how he was in love with me. He went on to state that he wanted to protect me, and was sorry that he acted like that, but he couldn't deal with seeing me with another man. He even stated that he used to sneak and watch me and his uncle have sex when he was younger. It was all too much for me. I made him pack his things and I drove him back to Brooklyn. I dropped him off right where I picked him up from. I had no idea that he felt like that towards me. In my mind, he was my godson, but this man was obsessed with me and potentially dangerous. I wasn't scared of him. I was scared of what I would do to him if he tried to hurt me. It was creepy. When I dropped him off, he was still pleading with me. I just let him make a couple of phone calls and gave him a parting speech on his crazy behavior. I told him that I couldn't be around him if he felt those inappropriate feelings for me, and I wished him well. When I got back home, I felt a sense of relief and started cleaning my crib. The next morning, my daughter left for school, but suddenly ran back into the house. "MOMeeeee my God Brother is back!" she sing songed.

"HUH!?" I couldn't believe my ears. That nut job was back. He had the nerve to come all the way back to Connecticut on the train after I specifically told him that he couldn't stay with me any longer. I was steaming. I went to my door and there he was dressed in black from head to toe, looking like a madman with a puppy-dog expression on his face. I starting going off on him. He just went down into my basement where the laundry room is set up for the building. He actually stated that he wasn't leaving, and he would sleep down there. By then, I was near hysteria. I was so f***ing mad. I felt a fury so deep that if I would have had a gun, I would have definitely shot him just for the brazen nerve he possessed.

I started pulling his suitcase up the stairs and he pulled my hand away from it. That was it! We started tussling and, of course, I had no wins against his big ass, so I stopped. He wasn't being aggressive. He was trying to restrain me, which made me even madder. At that point, I just said the hell with it, and told him that the police in my neighborhood would lock him up for trespassing, so he had to leave my building. He was just standing there like a zombie. I realized that he was high, because there were no getting through to him, and he wasn't leaving. That's when I left, figuring once he saw me drive off, he would go to the train station like any normal person, and head on back to wherever his ride took him. There was no such luck. While I was driving, I get a call about twenty minutes later from my ADT Security system operator. She told me that my alarm system had been set off and there was an intruder in my home. My heart dropped and I told her to call the cops. By the time I got back, the police were there, but my godson was nowhere to be found. After explaining the situation to the police, they had a clear understanding that he was obsessed with me and wouldn't take no for an answer. I wanted him arrested. Plain and simple! I didn't trust him. I had to protect myself and my daughter, or I would be back in prison for killing that maniac.

The police started a manhunt for him and canvassed my neighborhood. It wasn't going to be hard to find a dark-skinned male around 6'2", who dressed in all black in my predominately white neighborhood. Sure enough, he was spotted about twenty minutes later. He had the nerve to come strolling down the block like nothing ever happened. I knew right then and there that homie was a problem. He lied to the police right in front of my face, and told them I let him in my apartment. I spazzed hard on him right in front of the cops. **"B***h, I let you in!? You lying piece of shit! LOOK ME IN MY EYES AND TELL ME THAT!"** I roared. It must have registered to him that I was just as crazy as he was, because he dropped his head and admitted that he climbed through my window to put his bags down. That was his lame excuse. He stated that he didn't take anything, and he just wanted to put his belongings back in my house; even though I told him that he couldn't stay. 'Ain't that a b***h? I had had enough of his demented behind. I told the police that I was pressing charges and I wanted him arrested. Call me a snitch, rat or whatever, but that negro was going to jail. See, I had to do what society required me to do, because I have changed my life. I will always be an O.B.G at heart, but my mind is matured. I knew that if I didn't have him locked up, I would have done something to that boy. I would have been the one cuffed in that cruiser instead of him. That's real talk. I had to get an Order of Protection against him, and I pray that he doesn't violate the order.

He did sixty days in jail and was released. The D.A. on his case contacted me before his sentencing and asked me did I want him to do a year followed by three years of probation. My bleeding-heart self said no. I made a plea for him to come home because I thought that he learned his lesson that NO MEANS NO! Unfortunately, his love for me turned into hate, and now he threatens me daily. He stalks me on all of my internet sites. I block him, but he finds a way to pop back up. I changed my phone number, but he got the new one. He texts me and leaves me menacing threats on my voicemail stating "I'm going to burn you and your grandmother's house down." That really bothered me because why my 87 year old Nana? What did I do to him to make him hate me this much?

I asked him that and guess what he said? He wants me to buy him a Protools program so he can make music, but I'm hating on him, and I don't want to see him become successful. Go figure! The lesson I learned from this experience is you can never do enough for a person. They will always forget about all the times you said "yes". It's the first time you say "no' that defines you. I also learned that I can't personally help people anymore. When I want to help a cause, it will be through my charities. I will have my handlers deal with the people, because I seem to attract the crazies. If it's not a child or a senior citizen, I will not let them into my personal space. I have a genuine fear of humans from all of my negative experiences.

I am a recovering addict. My addiction is money and violence. Any sort of negative situation, like the ones I have described in length, will trigger my thirst for revenge. It's best for me to live in peace and harmony, while staying away from people, places and things that bring me harm. I see why celebrities don't hang out with people who are not in their circle. It's so hard to get into their loop because they have to be very wary of people. It's always a hidden agenda or a motive behind someone's intentions, which makes it hard for the few humans who are genuine and sincere to infiltrate the successful society. You have to really prove yourself. I never understood that until I realized that it is impossible to "keep it real" with the hood, because if you don't have what I have, then nine times out of ten, you want it. So, when you get in a certain tax bracket, you have to move and hang around folks who got it like you do. My only problem is that I love the 'hood. I love my people, and I find a lot of phoniness in the Industry. I also suffer from a bleeding heart complex. I want to help the world, but I always wind up helping the wrong folks. I can't win for losing!

My entire life has been full of pain and negativity. I just want to be happy. I control my own destiny and, as long as I stay focused, I will win. I am a product of my choices, not my environment. I chose my path in life, and I got the hand that was dealt to me. My sister had the same addict for a mother, and her father was a dope fiend just like mines. He also died from cancer when she was younger. He was never in her life, but through all of those adversities, she became successful. She graduated from two Ivy League Universities: Hunter College and Columbia University. She obtained a Master's Degree in Social Work, which proves my point that it's the choices you make in life that will make or break you. Let my story be a lesson to the children coming up, who want to live that glamorous, hustling lifestyle, along with the children who have addicts for parents or no parents at all. Don't be a victim of circumstances, be a champion by choice. I still have a lot of living to do. I won't spend it by trying to beat the system, because I'll only beat myself. I pray that my career takes off and this book is the catalyst to my success. Most of all, I pray that someone who needed to read my story gets a message from it. I wrote it to save a life not to glorify mines.

Chapter Fourteen

I MISS YOU MAMA

It's obvious what this chapter is about. I miss my mother so much that it physically hurts sometimes. I would take her back right now, cracked out and all. It's nothing like having a mother to depend on, to share your problems with, and to love you like no other being on this earth. I always feel like she is reincarnated inside of my daughter. I based that on the little signs that I've noticed when my baby was younger. My mother used to suck her thumb sideways, which totally embarrassed me whenever she did it in public. One day, when Velvet was about one year old, she suddenly stuck her thumb in her mouth sideways. She did it exactly how my mother used to do it. Up until then, Velvet had never sucked her thumb. Plus, it was no way for her to have mimicked another baby, because I had never seen another person suck their finger in that odd manor. In addition, she used to grab my mother's picture and kiss it. She had never seen her in person, and couldn't even talk, but she seemed to know that was her grandmother. She also has my mom's eyes. The way she loves me, along with our close bond, makes me feel my mother's spirit is in her.

Since the death of my mom, it has been very hard on me. The pain never stops. The day she died, I received a call from her mother, my nana, informing me that I needed to come to the hospital because my mother was dying. I had been absent from the hospital for a couple of days because my mother was dying. I couldn't take seeing her like that. The AIDS virus had weakened her immune system and her T-cell count was nonexistent, meaning her body had stopped fighting the virus. She was 88 pounds and looked skeletal. I didn't want to remember her like that. Back then, the doctors would make visitors wear scrubs and surgical mask to protect the patient from whatever germs we may have. It made my mom feel like she was an alien and very contagious. I hated it! I made her feel good because I was never afraid to touch her. She knew that people were terrified of catching the dreaded disease. Back then, no one knew enough about it, so they were weary that it would spread easily. I was fiercely protective over her, and would go ham if people acted funny around her. I put ointment on her lesions and bathed her. She was my mother and, as far as I was concerned, I wasn't scared of what she had. I wanted to die with her. I felt so sorry for her, and would put up a brave front for her, but I would cry my heart out when I wasn't around her. It broke me to see her in that condition. She had every infection that was associated with that disease. Her mouth was always filled with thrush, which is a yeast infection that develops in the mouth of people who are infected with HIV or AIDS. It was a very disturbing sight, but she was my mommy, and I didn't care. That's why I am so health conscience. I encourage the young people who I speak with to use protection if they are sexually active. I saw the effects of AIDS up close and personal. It is horrible. Today, people have a chance to live with the disease due to all the new and improved medications, but when my poor mother contracted the virus, it was deadly.

Kids today are having sex at a very young age, just like I started out, so I know what I am talking about. You can't rely on a boy to protect you, so it's important for females to have condoms available; that way, you can protect yourself. In a perfect world, girls would wait until they were married to have sex, but realistically, it's happening at very tender ages. My daughter is eleven years old, and she knows everything there is to know about puberty and sex, because I don't want her to learn anything from the street. She knows how her grandmother died, and that made her very aware of the sexually transmitted diseases that can destroy your body and possibly kill you. I have a lot of tattoos, but I make sure that I watch the artist change the needle. My mother could have possibly contracted the disease from an unsanitary needle that she shared with another heroin user. I do not want to die like my mother, who was riddled with disease. It was inhumane. In all reality, it could have been avoided if she had simply protected herself. On her death bed, she used her last breath to tell me to always take care of my sister. Her regret in life was not being a good mother to us, and especially not bonding with her youngest daughter. She always told me, "I lost Rocki, but I still have you, Toki." I would try to convince her that my little sister still loved her, but she just didn't know her like I did. The first year of a child's life is the bonding period, and my mother did that with me. However, she gave my sister to my godmother too early, and the bonding wasn't complete. Simple as that! I didn't have this wisdom when my mom died, so I actually made my sister feel real bad at the funeral. I accused her of not loving our mommy. I wigged out because I felt she didn't show enough grief, and I took all of my pain out on her. That is something that we never discuss to this day. I am taking this opportunity to apologize to her, because she dealt with the pain her way. I know that my sister loved our mother. Unfortunately, she wasn't around our mother as much as I was, so she didn't have an opportunity to bond like I did. I cried for my mother all the time.

After she died, it was like a piece of my heart was ripped out. She died, on the 4th of July and, up until this day I don't like the celebration and fireworks.

It disturbs me that everyone is so happy on what was the saddest day of my life.

I also miss my godmother tremendously. She loved me so much that she tried to protect me from the outside by preventing me from going out there and having a normal childhood. I was so resentful that I couldn't go out and play with my friends that I held a grudge against my godmommy, but when my baby needed me most, I was there. She suffered from Alzheimer's disease. I was able to take care of her for five years before she died at the ripe old age of 92. She was a feisty old lady, and I loved her dearly. She no longer knew who I was, but she felt my love. After fighting with her to bathe her in the tub, she would always hug me and say, "You're a nice lady. Thank you." Those simple words of gratitude would let me know that she felt my love for her. I will never forget the one time, out of five years, when she had a moment of clarity and called me by my name. I burst into tears of joy and smothered her with kisses. I couldn't believe it! Just like the scene in my favorite movie, "The Note Book", I had a few moments to speak with her, and she knew exactly who I was. I kept telling her over and over that I loved her and appreciated her for taking care of me and my sister and that I would always take care of her. Then she was gone. Again!

Caring for a person who suffers from Alzheimer's requires a lot of patience and love, because the patient reverts back into a toddler. They have no idea how to feed or bathe themselves correctly, and they need twenty-four hour care. When I had to go out, I would hire personal friends that I could trust to care for her. I want to take the time to thank Margaret "Poochie" Monroe for being one of those people who loved my godmother, and made sure that she was cared for while I was in the streets making money to supply all of her needs. She didn't have insurance, so there was no health coverage to hire a home attendant.

My girlfriend, Goldie, who I was dealing with at the time, also took care of my mommy (what I called my darling) for me when I had to do seven months in jail. I love her to this day for that, she made sure she was straight, and I didn't have to worry about her. The conditions I found mommy in when I came home from my first bid were horrifying. She was literally sleeping in her own feces. She was left alone in her apartment to fend for herself by her daughter. I immediately moved in with her, and renovated her place, and brought my darling back to life. I know in my heart that I am blessed now because of that. She is an angel on my right shoulder, and my mom sits perched on my left one. Both of them guide me through life and protect me from harm.

I will never forget the day I needed my angels the most. I was in a night club. I went to the bathroom and in walked this dude named Money. He was Larrel's cousin. Not only was he related to the guy who I shot, but he thought that I had him shot up while he was holding his son. A few weeks after I shot Larrel, my homie CB, my friend Pam and I went to Farragut. I was selling some clothes, while CB and Pam were chilling with me in my car. I saw Money and asked him did he know anybody that wanted to buy my merchandise. He loved to crack jokes and started kidding around with me. I let my guard down. He took me to another booster's crib, which I thought was very strange. Of course, she didn't buy anything because she got her clothes for free the same way I got mines, so that made me wonder why Money wasted my time taking me to see her. I found out when I got back down stairs. CB was fuming when I got to the car. Him, and Pam had been robbed. They got jacked for their jewelry and all the stolen goods in my trunk. I immediately put two and two together. Money had us setup. CB and Pam were casualties of the Jack, because the heist was only intended for me. It was in retaliation of Larrel getting shot. We found out later that Money was related to him. So naturally, CB being who he was wanted revenge. They basically messed up when they involved him and his girl.

The next week, Money got shot up in broad daylight, while holding his son. He was almost killed, and fortunately his son wasn't harmed. The night in the club was the first time I bumped into Money after a year, and it wasn't a family reunion.

I came out of the bathroom stall and, there he was, standing in the woman's bathroom with a sinister look on his face. I almost shitted on myself, but I played it cool. I thought to myself, this nicca is gonna' clap me. I regretted getting caught slipping (without my gun). "What's up, Money?" I said coolly. He had his hands in his pockets and gave me a head nod. I put my hands in my pocket, bluffing like I had my gat on me, and stared him down. "That's fucked up what happened, but you should have never got involved in that shit with your cousin. Niccaz ain't playing out here. It's real in the field!" I said, rationalizing the street justice that went down. I was scared, but he didn't know it. I was acting like I was ready for whatever. I didn't know if I was going to leave that bathroom alive, but I wasn't going out like a coward. It worked because he started copping a plea (explaining his version of what happened and denied any involvement in the robbery). He told me that he didn't want any problems. He had almost died and he wasn't involved in the madness. "Whew!" I realized that I had the upper hand. He only wanted to talk to me, hoping that I would relay the message to CB that he didn't want any beef with him. I don't know if he had a gun on him and just had a change of heart or whatever, but I am blessed. I could have been a goner, but I was prepared to meet my maker, and my mother.

I lived my life recklessly and lawlessly; therefore, I felt that whatever happens in that bathroom that night was repercussions of how I lived. The fact that I am still here to talk about it is proof that I'm here for a reason.

Now that leaves me with one more memory to share. I can't close this chapter without talking about my father. Coydine Mackie was absent my entire childhood and teen years because of his drug addiction and periods of incarceration. When he came home from his last bid, he made the choice to find me and apologize for his faults. He wanted to make it up to me. At that time, I was nineteen and incarcerated in Bay View Correctional Facility. I was very bitter towards him. To be honest, I had no interest in meeting him, and held him accountable for his actions. After I realized that he was persistent in his attempts to visit me, and he wasn't bullshitting, I let him come visit me. We had a long conversation. He explained to me about his life and the things he had been through. He didn't know how to be a father, mainly because his father wasn't around for him or his eight other siblings, leaving his mother to care for them alone.

He was a wild child, who started robbing and and stealing at the age of eleven in an attempt to bring money home to help his mother feed and clothe him and his brother and sisters. He started going to Juvenile Correctional Facilities, and never had a proper education or a chance at life. He told me about how he started shooting heroin, which was the drug of choice in the seventies for all the cool kids and hustlers who were in raised in the projects. He met my mother, who, at the time, was a good girl. He admitted to corrupting her and turning her on to the streets.

After I was conceived, he went to prison and held me for the first time when he came home from his bid. I was ten months old. That was the last time he'd seen me until that prison visit. He said he had started committing robberies in an attempt to provide for my mother and me, and immediately landed back in prison. It was a vicious cycle that brought tears to my eyes as I listened to his story. In total my father spent 29 years of his life in prison. I was sitting in jail, meeting him for the first time, and it hit me like a ton of bricks. My mother was dead! All I had was my dad, who finally got his life together and wanted to make amends with me. I hugged him, letting him know that I had forgiven him, and we've been close ever since. I am proud to say that he has remained clean and sober and crime free.

I can't end my story without talking about my maternal grandmother. She is all I have left in my family. God has blessed me and my sister with our Nana. I held a grudge against her when I was younger, and it caused us not to get along. She never knew this, but my mother told me that the reason why she ran to the streets and started getting high was because her mother didn't show her enough love. She was a great provider because both of her children were well taken care of, but she wasn't affectionate. My mother yearned for love and attention, but she didn't get it from home, so she turned to the streets. It's a common tale, so I want to say this: If you have a child, it is your responsibility to nurture that child with love and affection. Love is a powerful emotion, and it will cure the evils of the world. I kiss my daughter and tell her that I love her everyday even when she gets on my nerves. I think of all the time that I yearned for her, and I thank God I am able to be with her.

I also held a grudge against my nana because I felt that she should have took us in, instead of letting us go to my godmother. There was no reason why she didn't step up to the plate, but I am so happy that she didn't because my godmother was the most loving person in the world. I was blessed to have been raised by the Robinson family. After all the pain, anger and depression that I went through, I started to remember all the love that they gave me throughout my childhood. That is part of why I am so nurturing and loving now. I want to love all the hurting children in the world. Adults are set in their ways, but we can save the children. Both of my nana's children died from the AIDS virus at very young ages, my mother was 36 years old, and my uncle, Kevin Williams, was 42 years old. They were both intravenous drug users, searching for love in all the wrong places.

When I listen to this song, "I Miss You Mama", I cry and my heart aches for my mother and the life she lived. I wish that I could rewind the hands of time for my family. We represent a portion of the world who struggle with poverty, drugs and crime. Both of my parents and I have spent large portions of our lives in prison. In addition we have used drugs and abused others. On paper, we look like the scum of the earth, and that is how society judges us. I hope by sharing my life, it will explain how we got there, and how our choices changed us. My mother's choice destroyed her life. My dad finally made a choice, which changed his destiny and saved his life. I am a work in progress. I am making the choice by revealing to the world the Tales of an Original Bad Girl. I choose to live and die righteously. I want to break my family's cycle of destruction and pave the path for my daughter. Her parents are ex-cons, but we both have made the choice to change. Her dad has successfully remained out of prison, and has been employed since she was born. I applaud him for that and, although we have had our differences we have come together as a family unit to raise our child. We are not in a relationship, but we put our daughter first. He and her, spend time together on alternate weekends. She bonds with him and it makes her happy. He has provided for her financially on his own, without any prodding from the courts, and I commend him for that. He helped me out a great deal since I have been home. I know I describe him as a lunatic, but that was when we were both nut jobs.

He has changed and became a decent human being. My daughter asked him one day, "Why did you hit Mommy?" He paused and, after really thinking about it, told her that he actually didn't know why. That answer was honest and forthright, which satisfied her and me. He didn't deny it or justify it. He was bewildered by his actions. No one knows what makes a person do certain things until they know themselves. I know why I lived like I did and I know why I changed. People can change. That is what I want the judicial system to realize, so they can stop judging me or others like me from our past mistakes. If you ask anyone who knows me, they will tell you I am the most loyal, kind, loving and generous person they know. If you see my rap sheet, you may think I am dangerous, untrustworthy and a very bad person. I have changed, and so can you. No one is perfect but God. So, before you judge a book by its cover, read "my" story.

THE END

Grab A Copy of Mack Mama's Latest Title: "Daisy Jones"
Now Available on Amazon
http://www.amazon.com/Daisy-Jones-ebook/dp/B005IZALV0/ref=sr_1_1?ie=UTF8&qid=1338987213&sr=8-1

Star Status Publishing
P.O Box 237
Derby, Connecticut 06418
mackmama1@gmail.com

Tales of an Original Bad Girl...............................15.95
Shipping and handling...4.95
Total..20.90

Checks or Money Orders

Purchaser Information

Name...

Address..

City.. State...............
Zip.....................

        Quantity.................

Orders shipped directly to Correctional Facilities will receive 25%
off of the sales price courtesy of Mack Mama

Tales of Original Bad Girl................................11.97

Shipping and handling......................................3.20

Total...15.17

If your facility allows Cds check here.......Soundtrack won't

be included if you don't check the line. thanks!

TALES OF AN
ORIGINAL
BAD GIRL
AN **AUTOBIOGRAPHY**

▼ Now Available

This is the original cover for my book that I decided to change. I didn't want this cover to misrepresent the message that I want to relay by telling my story. I got to admit that I loved this cover, but some people let the image of me holding the guns, distract them from the inspirational words behind the cover. ▶

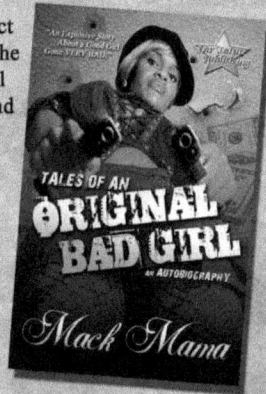

This is a toned down version of my story with the same shock value that the youth need in order to pay attention and learn from my mistakes. ▼

Mack Mama and Dashawn Taylor ▲
Author & C.E.O of HotBookCovers.com
He does all of my Fabulous Covers!

Sparkles & Mack Mama at my ▶
1st book release party.

◀ Chloe and Mack Mama

Mack Mama and Chloe's ▶
beautiful daughter… they look
like sisters.

Brooklyn's Finest: Monique, NeNe, ▶ Mack and Diane

◀ Brooklyn Love & Support from my home girl Diane

Me in the booth doing what I love to do, spitting that FIRE! MUSIC is my lover that makes me feel good and Books is my ▶ Husband that pays the bills. I'm always cheating with my lover. lol

Mack and Sparkles at a Book Signing

Me in front of Déjà vu Book Lounge with Author/Owner Deborah "Sexy" Cardona

Lisa Evers and Mack Mama in the HOT 97.1FM STUDIO Preparing for an episode of Street Soldiers.

The Legendary Omar Tyree and Mack Mama

D-Block Artist/Author Styles P and Mack Mama ▶

D-Block Artist/Author Styles P .... Nuff Said!

Me at a Booksigning Event ▶

◀ I love my readers!

My future stars.
Sparkles' son Seth and
My little me Velvet on ▶
the grind.

Mr. Cheeks reppin' Mack Mama. ▶

◀ The Green-Eyed Bandit
Erick Sermon and Me

Mack Mama and ▶
"No Malice" a.k.a
Malice from the rap
group The Clipse

A few of my favorite pics of me!

The God M.C Rakim ▶
and Mack Mama

Mack Mama and Berry...
Brooklyn's Finest

Mo Mo B, Chloe, Mack ▶
and Rocki my sissy.

◀ I love my readers and
they love me.

Me and my lovely sister Raquele (Ivy League college graduate with her ▶ Masters Degree in Social Work....lol...she hates when I brag about her.)

◀ Author Treasure E. Blue and Mack Mama.

Me and My homie ▶ "TNT" from The Harlem Rockets

Mack Mama and
T.I. (The King) ▶

◀ Mack Mama and Brian "Baby"
Williams #CashMoney

Trey Songz and Mack Mama...
he is such a sweetheart. ▶

Kevin Liles and Mack
Mama. I'm surrounded by
so much power! This is the
power page for sure. I only
pray that some of that
magnetic chemistry rubs
off on me.

Mack Mama and
Ronald "Slim" Williams
#CashMoney

Wahida Clark (My inspiration
…love her!) and Mack Mama ▶
at her "Payback A'int Enough"
Book Release Party
#CashMoneyContent

Kanye West and ▶
Mack Mama.

Mack Mama,
Author/Publisher
DC Bookdiva and ▶
Author Nene Capri

◀ Mack Mama and Jim Slice from
Flashback Fever Radio. Check
out the interview on my
youtube channel (mackmama1)

Mack Mama and Salaudin ▶
Rose on the set of a video
shoot I appeared in. Check
it out on youtube (Broken
Genius Films)

Mack Mama and
Tiny (Xscape).
She is such a darling. ▶

◀ Me and Kandi Burress
(Atlanta Housewives,
Xscape)

Mack Mama with
Newscaster from
Channel 7 ▶

Me in my favorite colors.
▶

◀ Me in my favorite colors in
2004 when my stomach was
flat enough to show my
"Mack Mama Tat". I'm
gonna' get that back lol

I rep O.B.G. Hard!
(Original Bad Girl) ▶

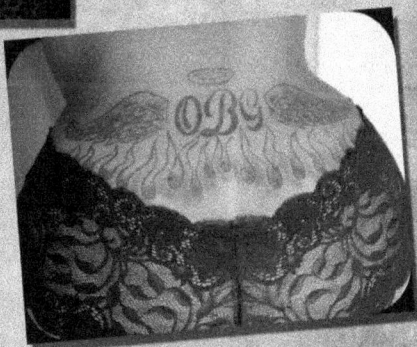

222

◀ At the casino bringing in the New Year. Happy, free and making money.

More love and support. ▶

◀ R.I.P Unique

www.ingramcontent.com/pod-product-compliance
Lightning Source LLC
Chambersburg PA
CBHW051952090426
42741CB00008B/1364